THE
MARSHLAND
WORLD

THE MARSHLAND WORLD

RON WILSON
PAT LEE

BLANDFORD PRESS
Poole   Dorset

First published in the U.K. 1982 by Blandford Press,
Link House, West Street, Poole, Dorset, BH15 1LL

Distributed in the United States by
Sterling Publishing Co. Inc.,
2 Park Avenue, New York, N.Y. 10016

British Library Cataloguing in Publication Data

Wilson, Ron
  The marshland world.
  1. Marsh ecology
  I. Title
  574.5′26325   QH104

ISBN 0 7137 1199 X

Designed by Richard Johnson

Phototypeset by Oliver Burridge Filmsetting Ltd
Printed by Tonbridge Printers Ltd

CONTENTS

ILLUSTRATIONS

The authors and publisher gratefully acknowledge the following for permission to reproduce photographic material.

Colour

Alan Beaumont: pp. 96 and 97; R. Burt/Martin King and Mike Read: p. 85; N. R. Caulton/NHPA: p. 76; J. M. Combes/Martin King and Mike Read: pp. 88 (*top*) and 101 (*top*); Geoff Doré/Martin King and Mike Read: pp. 36 (*bottom*), 48 (*bottom*), 89 (*bottom*) and 105; Robin Fletcher: pp. 1, 40 (*bottom*), 41 (*bottom*), 44 (*top*), 52 (*top and centre*), 53 (*top and centre*), 56 (*bottom*), 57 (*bottom*), 61 (*top and bottom*), 80, 81, 88 (*bottom*), 89 (*top and centre*), 92 and 101 (*bottom*); J. Green: p. 53 (*bottom*); Eric Hosking: pp. 125 (*bottom*) and 128 (*top*); E. A. Janes/NHPA: p. 73; Martin King and Mike Read: pp. 33, 37 (*bottom*), 40 (*top*), 45 (*bottom*), 52 (*bottom*), 60 (*top and bottom*), 64, 68, 108, 109, 112, 113, 117, 121, 124 (*top and bottom*), 125 (*top*), 128 (*bottom*) and 129 (*top and bottom*); Pat Lee: pp. 4, 21, 28, 36 (*top*), 37 (*top*), 44 (*bottom*), 49 (*top and bottom*), 56 (*top*) and 57 (*top*); Audley Money-Kyrle: pp. 45 (*top*), 48 (*top*) and 88 (*centre*).

Black and white

Robin Fletcher: p. 79 (*bottom*); Eric Hosking: pp. 72, 76, 107, 115 (*top*) and 119; Martin King and Mike Read: p. 145; Pat Lee: pp. 8, 9 (*left and right*), 10 (*top and bottom*), 11, 12, 13, 14 (*top and bottom*), 15, 17, 18 (*top and bottom*), 22, 23, 26, 29 (*bottom*), 74, 106, 111, 115 (*bottom*), 133, 135, 136 and 138; Roger Lee: p. 29 (*top*); Audley Money-Kyrle: pp. 77, 81, 92 and 93; Norwich Central Library/Norfolk County Council: pp. 19 and 25; Laurence Perkins: pp. 79 (*left and top right*) and 95; Press-tige Pictures Ltd: pp. 134, 139 and 141.

ACKNOWLEDGEMENTS

I AM GRATEFUL TO a number of people who have assisted in one way or another during the course of the writing of this book. Anne Dyer provided some information on basketry; Nancy Lee Child (Handweavers Studio and Gallery Ltd) suggested some useful contacts, as did Anne French, Information Officer of the Crafts Council; several members of the Nature Conservancy Council made helpful suggestions or gave details of contacts, including N. English, P. J. Horton, Harold Dollman and R. A. Lindsay. Members of CoSIRA (in Norwich and Salisbury) answered queries, as did the Wildfowl Trust and the International Waterfowl Research Bureau, WAGBI (now the British Association for Shooting and Conservation), Dr Ted Ellis, Tony Cook (Wildfowl Trust, Peakirk), Chris Harbard (Information Officer, RSPB) and Mr A. V. Mindham.

Pat Lee has supplied many notes and also read the typescript, correcting the errors. However, any inaccuracies which remain are my own and I accept responsibility for them.

Finally my thanks to Beth Young, Group Editor at Blandford Press for her help, encouragement and gentle chiding at all times.

PREFACE

LIKE MANY OTHER HABITATS the marshland is a fascinating place: there are bird species which are found in no other areas, plants have become specially adapted to deal with the prevailing conditions and the whole community forms the basis for a unique study.

Since this book is called *The Marshland World*, it is appropriate that we should look at the marsh in relation to the areas around it, which, although not strictly 'marsh', are part of the marshland world. Thus the animals, including fish, which live in the marshland waters are described, as are those plants which live in aquatic conditions.

In dealing with marshland plants, it is difficult to draw a line and people visiting the area will be just as intrigued by those plants growing in the water as by those living on the land.

To look merely at the wildlife of the marsh would be to do the area an injustice. Several crafts have evolved particularly around some of the plants which are found in the marsh and these are dealt with. In the past, people living in such places have had to struggle against tremendous difficulties. The wild-fowler of old was not only obtaining a living, but often had to do so in atrocious conditions.

Marshland craft, especially developed for navigating in swamplike conditions, as well as in open water, provide an interesting glimpse into a virtually forgotten way of life, especially in the highly technological twentieth century.

We have tried to look at as many different aspects of the area as possible and, although, inevitably, some things may have been omitted, we hope to have given a balanced view of *The Marshland World*.

Ron Wilson
Weedon 1982

viii

INTRODUCTION TO THE MARSHLAND
What is a marsh?

ALTHOUGH THE QUESTION, 'What is a marsh?' might seem a simple one, in strict ecological terms it is difficult to define clearly the term 'marsh'.

In the true marsh, the soil is constantly waterlogged. In the summer, the water level, which is then at its lowest, is just below the soil surface. Indeed, it seldom rises above the soil surface at any time in the year. The soil has an inorganic (i.e. mineral) basis, usually silt or clay, in contrast to the soil of the fens which consists of organic peat. However, much marshland soil contains rich peaty deposits.

In days gone by, marshes covered much larger areas than they do today, but vast tracts have been destroyed by extensive drainage schemes, aimed at reclaiming the soil, mainly for agricultural purposes. The largest expanses of marsh are in the lowland areas of Europe, although they do occur in upland regions. There are many more plant species in the true marsh than in the reed-swamp and it is this variety that gives the marsh its characteristic flora.

The marsh is generally considered to be an area next to water—whether pond, lake or river—where the soil, although visible, is waterlogged just below its surface. Plants which grow there have roots which are adapted for conditions in which they are permanently covered with water. Marshy conditions, i.e. where the soil is waterlogged, may occur in a number of habitats, such as fen and bog, and even in certain areas of woodland.

There is a strange enchantment in the marshland world. It is a habitat which few people really know because it is so difficult to investigate.

Geologists will explain that a marsh forms where there is a depression in the land. If the depression is deep enough and if there is sufficient rainfall and drainage from higher ground, a lake normally results, but if the depression is too shallow for this, a marsh develops. Other marshes may form off the low-lying banks of rivers and lakes, where a typical marshland flora often begins to develop. In areas where there is a high rainfall, marshland may form in areas where drainage is slow.

In looking at the marshland world, it would be inappropriate to confine our attention simply to the reed-bed and reed-swamp zones, and to do so would lead to an incomplete understanding of the processes involved. The marsh has evolved from a more aquatic situation. As silt builds up around plants growing in the water, the level of the substrate is raised. The plants which are able to colonise such a habitat are different from those which grow in open water. Such a process is very slow.

Once marshland has been established, changes will gradually take place in the zones bordering it and, from the reed-swamp situation, silting gradually leads to the formation of dry land and, ultimately, in theory at least, to the climax vegetation which is alder carr.

To give some idea of interdependence and the processes which go on in such an area, *The Marshland World* looks at the whole area loosely termed 'marsh'.

The marsh, like any other habitat, is dynamic; in many instances perhaps more so than any other habitat. There is a four-fold cycle in the marsh. Created in a flood, it flourishes, evolves and then dies. Deposition of material in a river can result in the formation of a marsh, but continued deposition from the same source can cause its death. The process is not instantaneous, but spans a long period of time.

Drainage

EARLY DRAINAGE OF THE MARSHES by wind pumps, and later by steam pumps, was carried out to preserve the old grazing marshes, and did not harm the habitat, a fact borne out by the richness of the flora and invertebrate fauna of many of these early drainage channels or *dykes*. Derelict pumps, many of which have been preserved, serve as a monument to this era in the past life of the marsh.

The earlier marshman had a feeling for his work. Using specialised hand-made tools—*cromes, dydles, meags* and *shore knives*—he kept the dykes clean. Indeed, dyking was an important part of the marshland way of life.

Marshes were also drained in earlier times to combat the scourge of malaria. Mosquitoes bred in the often stagnant or slow-moving waters of the marsh. Drainage was seen as the only course of action, not only in tropical regions, but also in parts of Europe.

As the demand for more farmland in many parts of Europe became increasingly acute, the only remaining unproductive tracts left were extensive areas of wetlands. Along the coast these included salt marsh and brackish marsh: further inland there were areas of freshwater marsh and grazing meadows.

Seen by many people as dark, wet and unpleasant wildernesses, many of the inhabitants of the marshes probably rejoiced that large areas of useless land were to be reclaimed. Productive fields of celery, wheat and sugar beet now flourish where once the tall 'unproductive' reeds dominated the landscape.

Even if drainage has not taken place, these marshland areas are still subject to other pressures, including eutrophication and pollution (see p. 5). Recreation also takes its toll by increasing the disturbance to an area.

Many problems have been caused unintentionally. Where marshland waterways have been altered to improve navigation, the characteristic flora and, to some extent, the fauna has invariably been changed. Research has shown that, over the last 20 to 25 years, there has been a decrease in the number and variety of marshland plants and animals. Studies have shown that the drainage of marshes has produced unforeseen side effects. Where marshes are reclaimed and the waterways canalised, more water drains off than is necessary, resulting in a loss of productivity due to the drying-out of the soil. Cumulative effects can be seen: the soil breaks down and erosion is increased. In extreme cases, a transition to desert-like terrain may occur.

Wetlands have an important role to play, which extends far beyond the immediate areas which they cover. Research, although still in its infancy, indicates that wetland habitats such as marshes have a number of hitherto ignored or misunderstood functions. Where tracts of marshland border river valleys, they form part of nature's safety system. After heavy rain, when torrents of water make their way hurriedly down river in their eager race to the sea, flooding occurs. The marsh quickly and effectively soaks up and holds excess water like a gigantic sponge, to release it at a later stage. Wetland areas are also responsible for providing a supply of underground water.

Drainage reverses this natural safety valve, often causing flooding of the

Drainage pumps, now a thing of the past in most marshland areas because of modern drainage methods, were necessary to keep the marshes drained.

farmland which has replaced the marsh and sometimes destroying valuable crops.

Many groups of animals have suffered as a result of pressure on, or a reduction in, marshland areas. Insects, including the beautiful dragonflies, have decreased in numbers because of the demise of many of their former haunts. Receding marshland areas have reduced the numbers of aquatic species and many water bugs and beetles have suffered.

Undoubtedly one of the most noticeable declines has been in the number of amphibians—the frogs, toads and newts. Without water no eggs can be laid and the life cycle cannot be completed.

Where marshland areas are not being reclaimed, it often happens that the water table becomes lower, often because of drainage in areas outside the habitat. Where this happens many of the typical moisture-loving plants are eradicated, the area changes and a less interesting and less varied flora results. Coarser vegetation dominated by tree species, such as sallow, replaces the smaller herbs.

There is no doubt that wetland habitats, like marshes, harbour a wide range of species unique to each haunt. In some cases it may be a species as large as the bittern, or a flower as small as the water violet. As we lose such species, man's wildlife heritage is devalued.

Managing the marshland

THE TURNING POINT in an understanding of the importance of wetlands came as a result of the 1971 International Conference on the Conservation of Wetlands and Waterfowl held in Ramsar, Iran. The brief for the convention was to look at the problems which concerned wetland habitats on a worldwide basis. The strongest recommendation from the Conference was that major wetland habitats should be conserved. The Conference covered all wetlands and included freshwater marshes, as well as coastal ones, flood meadows as well as fen.

Apart from some large-scale drainage of marshland areas, much work was piecemeal in earlier times, leaving small often isolated areas of marsh. Although some of these smaller areas were ultimately used for agriculture and for commercial development, many were used for the dumping of rubbish.

A complete understanding of the needs of any species is essential before management plans can be formulated and carried out and careful ecological surveys must be undertaken. The natural succession that takes place in the marshland habitat, which finally results in climax vegetation, must be taken into account.

Modern-day management needs to be carefully planned, because the use of contemporary dredging machines to clear out silted areas or for cutting back the waterside vegetation can be almost as damaging as using an area for the dumping of waste.

When marshland areas are opened up to the public, damage can be considerable. For example, when paths are put in, they may cause breaks in the water table, leading to an alteration of, or damage to, the zonation of vegetation.

Once drawn up, management plans which are then carried out at inopportune times can result in the complete loss of, for example, a generation of frogs, which rely on a regular cycle of events for their well-being.

One of the most difficult problems to control is eutrophication and pollution. Eutrophication results from an enrichment of the water to artificially high levels. The chemicals responsible for this are nitrates and phosphates. They reach the marsh in run-off water and in sewage effluent. Phosphates originate mainly from effluent, particularly from detergents, and nitrates mainly from fertilisers.

A combination of these elements leads to the intense growth of algae. In many cases, the growth is so rapid that the algae quickly form a thick layer on the surface, preventing the penetration of light to lower levels. This affects the growth of the large water plants which may eventually disappear, as has happened extensively in the Norfolk Broads. These occurrences can be prevented by removing phosphate from the effluent and the use of a phosphate stripper is being evaluated in East Anglia.

Where pesticides reach the water, they too can have disastrous effects, decimating the amphibian population and killing off large numbers of fish.

Drainage and intensive farming methods often bring about a lowering of the water table in the marshes, which may affect the zonation of plants, leading to a more rapid plant succession, with scrub covering extensive areas. To raise the water table again, either by flooding the area or by some artificial means (such as large-scale excavation) is extremely costly and therefore generally prohibitive. To maintain natural marshland conditions is difficult, because of the fluctuations due to the yearly cycle of events.

There is still a great deal which is not understood about marshes and this applies equally to methods of management and to the requirements of its inhabitants. To manage an area it is essential to understand as much as possible about the life history of any given species. But, even today, after prolonged study by many individuals, the information needed to manage intelligently the entire habitat of the marsh is sadly lacking.

PART I
MAN AND MARSHLAND
Crafts

IN THIS TECHNOLOGICAL AGE, crafts and craftsmen have taken a back seat and have a far less important role than in the past. Mass-produced articles have become the order of the day. But in the not-so-distant past, the craftsman was a very important person, particularly in the marshland. Fortunately the demand for his services is now on the increase, as people have come to realise how effective his skills can be. There are numerous small crafts associated with the marshland habitat and the materials which such an area produces, but in the space available we can only look briefly at some of the major ones.

In spite of the demand for such crafts, regretfully, with the ever-decreasing marshland habitat, it may not be too long before we lose, not the craftsmen, but the materials which they need. Any craftsman is dependent on certain raw materials to carry out his trade. The history of marshland crafts is a long one. Suffice it to say that man gradually came to realise that the objects around him could be used to his advantage and, by trial and error, he learned, for example, that certain twigs could be bent and fashioned to form baskets and that reeds could be used to thatch houses and produce a waterproof covering. As at present, some people showed a greater proficiency at a particular craft, resulting in differentiation of labour, each person providing a different service for his fellows.

REED HUSBANDRY
Undoubtedly the craft most often associated with marshland areas is thatching. There are two aspects of this craft: the thatching itself and the provision of a suitable supply of material. The cutting and harvesting of reed for thatching is still an important activity in many marshland areas. The reed used is *Phragmites australis*, (see p. 35) which, depending on its situation, grows to a height of between 150 and 300 cm (59 and 118 in). The plant is generally grown from underground rhizomes. Reed favours any damp area, including the margins of lakes and suitable stretches of rivers and streams. However, where it can be grown or controlled in large expanses, reed is a valuable crop.

In Britain, its chief value is as thatching material but, in other European countries where it is grown, it is an important raw material in the cellulose industry. It is also used to stabilise the banks of rivers and canals. Large areas of reed are found in Scandinavia and the Danube delta and, in the Netherlands, it has been used in the reclamation of the polders.

It is only in the British Isles that reed is important in thatching. It is also used, in a minor way, for temporary sheds, as fencing and to provide some protection to farm crops. In large reed-beds, the shoots may provide some fodder. In some countries, the rhizomes have been dug up and used to produce an alcoholic drink.

For good growth, the reed needs nutrient-rich soil, such as that in the

Reed fencing is used for both fences and buildings. Birdwatchers' hides constructed from reed fencing blend in well with the natural vegetation.

marshland area of East Anglia. Large areas of reed are found in Scotland, along the south coast of England and in south Wales, but the reeds will grow almost anywhere if conditions are suitable and reed-beds are widely distributed throughout Britain.

Because the best reeds have to be used, thatching is expensive, although a well-thatched roof will last for up to 80 years. When choosing his material, the thatcher will select both short and long bundles of reed, each of which is used for specific areas on the roof.

The hollow-stemmed reeds trap air and this gives them their good insulating properties. Reeds have been used for thatching for many centuries and Thomas Tusser commented on this in his *Five Hundred Points of Good Husbandry*, published in 1571, when he said, 'Where houses be reeded, as houses have need, Now pare off the moss, and go beat in the reed'.

Originally reeds were cut by each craftsman as he needed them, but at some stage it became apparent that management of the reed-beds was necessary and this is now practised in many areas. The reed-cutting season covers the period from just before Christmas to 5 April, at which time the reeds have lost their seeds and leaves—a stage called the *feather*. Growth is an important consideration in harvesting, which stops when the young shoots or *colts* push through the soil. Continued cutting will damage the colts, putting future crops at risk.

Some mechanisation has taken place in the harvesting of reeds. Motorised scythes are used, such as the Scandinavian Seiga harvester, which has wide tyres to prevent it from sinking in the soft reed-beds. Before mechanisation,

Hand-cutting of reeds was an essential feature of the marsh. Scythes were used and, despite the advent of machines, hand-cutting is still necessary where it is difficult to operate them, especially at the edges of marshes and in awkwardly-shaped areas.

Mechanised reed-cutting has speeded up the work. Although useful, these machines can only operate in areas where the substrate is firm.

reed-cutting was done by scythe and still is in some areas, especially where motor scythes cannot operate.

After cutting, the reed is cleaned with a reed-rake made from 6-in nails driven into a piece of wood. Unsuitable material, such as weeds and broken reed, is removed and the reed is then gathered into bundles. Each bundle is then bounced, butt down, onto a *bouncing* or *jouncing* board to level the ends and then tied about 30 cm (12 in) from the base. The bundles are then taken from the marsh by a boat—the reed-lighter—to be stacked close to a dyke or river ready for transportation.

The reed is sold in *bundles*. A standard-sized bundle, as defined by the Norfolk Reed Growers' Association, is 60 cm (24 in) in circumference at 30 cm (12 in) from the butt (lower end). A *fathom* consists of six standard bundles, measuring 180 cm (71 in) in circumference. A *long hundred* is 120 fathoms of reed (traditional).

Reed is cut either annually or biannually. Annual cutting is known as *single wale* and biannual cutting as *double wale*. More rarely there is a 3-year cycle, known as *triple wale*. Double wale is most common as biannual cutting not only increases the yield but also results in a more durable crop.

Correct management of the reed-beds is essential and waste and reed stubble is usually burnt. This kills off pests and weeds, while the ash puts back nutrients into the soil. New reed-beds are created by planting the rhizomes of *Phragmites australis*. Where seed is used, it is generally of Dutch origin, because seeds of British origin do not germinate successfully. Reeds grow best where the soil particles are of a fine texture; silt and silty peats

9

The reeds are bunched once they have been cut and, to prevent the reeds from falling out, each bunch is securely tied. The reeds are then bounced *to make sure that the ends of the stems are level.*

The reeds are carried off, ready to be transported.

Having been carried on a reed-lighter in the marshland waterways, the reeds are unloaded and stacked ready for further transportation or to be collected by the thatcher. It is important that the bundles are stacked correctly so that the rain will not soak into the reeds.

provide ideal growth conditions. Regular flooding replenishes the soil nutrients used by the growing plants.

The availability of water is very important. A continual supply is needed during the growing season, but dry conditions are desirable when the reeds are being cut. Such ideal conditions do not always occur, especially in marshland along river levels; here fluctuations in the level of the river water have the opposite effect, producing wet cutting seasons and dry growing seasons. In dry summers, invasion by weeds can be a nuisance.

This invasion of reed-beds by other species is a constant problem. The willow is usually the first species to appear, followed by grasses, such as *Agrostis stolonifera*, meadowsweet and willow herb. Willow herb is much disliked by the reed-cutters, because it is difficult to remove from the bunches. Management of reed-beds is therefore necessary to ensure a 'pure stand'.

The young reeds generally push through the soil in March, although they appear earlier if the winter is mild. During the winter, frost and trampling by men and animals may damage the reeds and, although many reeds recuperate, producing new buds, this results in a later crop. Growth is rapid at first, but decreases as the season progresses. Initial growth is fuelled by food stored in the rhizome and is helped by warm weather.

After early mild spells, frost is welcomed, as it arrests premature growth. When this happens, single buds may be replaced by two or three new ones, resulting in a much denser crop. Late frost, however, causes severe damage. Heavy late snowfalls may completely flatten the crop, in which case the reed has to be harvested early and burned, resulting in the loss of the crop.

Reeds flower either in late August or early September and the seeds ripen in November. The leaves of this perennial species then die; most have fallen off by Christmas, when harvesting begins.

There are few pests. The main enemies are caterpillars of *Arenostola phragmitidis* and *A. brevilinea*, which can damage the young reeds. *Liparia lucens* causes the common cigar gall and, although generally localised, it can be a nuisance. Young shoots may occasionally suffer from smut (*Ustilago grandis*), but the greatest problems are caused by the coypu (see p. 137), a rodent, introduced from Argentina some 70 years ago, whose activities turn the reed-beds into muddy quagmires.

THATCHING

Thatching, which has been practised for many centuries, is one of the oldest building crafts and has changed little since the Middle Ages. Apart from *Phragmites australis*, which is considered to be the prime thatching material, two other materials, *long straw* and *combed wheat reed*, are used. Long straw comes from wheat and must be wetted before use. Combed wheat reed, which is neither a straw nor a reed, is so-called because it has been passed through a comber.

Different materials have different life spans. Long straw lasts for between 10 and 20 years, combed wheat reed has to be replaced after 24 to 40 years

Once on the roof, the bundles of reeds are laid in by the thatcher and held in place by needles.

and reed may last for up to 80 years. Sedge, which is used on the ridge of the roof, needs renewing after 20 to 25 years.

The thatcher has a number of tools, most of which are hand-made. These and their uses are as follows:

a) *leggett* for dressing the reed into position,
b) *mallet* for driving in the spars,
c) *needles* for holding the bundles in position,
d) *knife* for cutting the bonds, etc,
e) *long eaves knife* for trimming the sedge and reed,
f) *shears* (the old-fashioned sheep shears) for trimming the reed.

Before a thatching job is begun, the reed is graded according to bunch length. It is carried out on site, and placed in three heaps of short, medium and long material respectively. Once sorted, up to six bunches at a time are then taken onto the roof. The first bunches are laid at the eaves and the leggett is used to dress these into position. They are held in place by a needle before being fixed with a hazel sway. The sways are placed 45 cm (18 in) apart and each is fastened either with an iron hook, made by the thatcher or a local blacksmith, or by tarred twine. A long needle is used to push the twine through the reed and around the rafter. Work progresses until the thatcher reaches the roof ridge.

He fashions the 10 cm (4 in) diameter ridge roll from coarser reed. Having made sure that the roll is long enough for the ridge, it is secured with twine at intervals of roughly 30 cm (12 in) before being attached to the ridge. The final bundles of reed are trimmed with a long eaves knife. The 30 cm (12 in) layer of reed which covers the ridge is then completed with a layer of sedge.

The thatcher can stamp his individuality on the roof when he completes

Initially, temporary sways, consisting of reeds, are used to hold the thatch in position. The thatch will only be fixed with permanent hazel sways when the thatcher is satisfied that he has positioned it correctly. For stability, these hazel sways are held in position with hooks driven through the thatch into the rafters.

Using a hand-made tool called a leggett, *the thatcher dresses the ends (butts) of the reed into the correct position.*

After the sedge has been placed on the ridge, the thatcher uses shears and other tools to finish off the ridge. Tie spars are used to hold the sedge in position. Long spars, called liggers, *run from one end of the roof to the other. Cross-rods are used to produce a pattern, individually worked out by each thatcher.*

the ridge because, although the ridge is sometimes left plain, it is more often decorated with a variety of patterns, including cross-sparring. In an ornamental ridge, the bottom edge is finished with a variety of shapes. Before the sedge is fixed, it will usually be soaked for a day to make it supple. Bunches of sedge, called *yealms*, are laid along the ridge with a good overhang. Spars are driven into the reed to hold the sedge in position. As further yealms are added, needles are used to hold them together. It is important that the thatcher gets each yealm close to the next one. Lengths of hazel or willow, called *spars* or *broaches* (*brotches*) hold the sedge in position. Broaches placed along the length of the ridge are termed *liggers* and those used for cross-pattern effects are called *cross-rods*.

The top ligger is arranged first and is secured with hazel staples, made from split hazel rods, bent over and twisted. These are driven in at a slight angle for added security. With all liggers in position, the cross-rods are fastened between them to form various patterns. Generally, each cross-rod is 15 cm (6 in) from its neighbour. Hazel staples are used to hold these in position.

Once the ridge material is in place, the thatcher tidies it up with a long eaves knife. If he wants a more decorative edge, he will use a shorter knife and his shears.

Recent developments have helped prolong the life of the thatch. Fine-gauge wire netting, particularly on the ridge, will prevent birds from making

Spars are generally fashioned from hazel rods. Here they are being prepared near the hazel coppice. Sometimes the job is carried out where the thatcher is working.

their nests in the reed and a copper strip 2·5 cm (1 in) wide, attached to the whole length of the ridge, will allow minute traces of copper to be released when it rains. This prevents the growth of algae and moss.

In addition to the thatch, the spars, liggers, cross-rods, sways and staples have to be obtained. Some come from the marsh, and hazel, which is preferable to willow, is obtained by coppicing trees. In the past, if not so much now, the thatcher would either have his own patch of coppice or have an arrangement for its supply.

Hazel needed for thatching has to be coppiced every 5 to 10 years. Once cut down to ground level, new shoots grow up from the stool, providing a supply of hazel rods, which are cut into 75 cm (30 in) lengths. These are often referred to as *gadds*, although Norfolk people call them broaches or brotches, and there are numerous other names from various parts of the country, e.g. *spies*, *roovers* and *scollops*.

BASKETRY

No one knows when man first learned to weave pliable stems, although archaeologists are certain that baskets have been made for at least 9000 years. The art of basketry has been adapted for a wide range of purposes, including roofs, doors and walls, as well as for a variety of containers. Basketry has also been used for producing sails, for making nets and fish traps, and also for rafts. At one time, it was used in the manufacture of ceremonial bowls for religious services.

Many attempts have been made to perfect basket-making machines which would produce large quantities of basketry more quickly than by hand, but to date this has been unsuccessful and all baskets depend on manual skills.

By experimenting with various materials, it was found that willow produced the best baskets. By cross-breeding willows, more pliable strains were developed and willow is now grown and managed specifically for craftwork.

Although most basket willows (osiers) used in Britain are grown here, some material is imported from other European countries, including France, Germany, Holland and Poland. If the willows do not grow 'naturally', they have to be cultivated in moist low-lying soils. Sites have to be large enough for fallow areas.

After deep-ploughing and manuring, the willows are planted from sets. Each set measures 30 cm (12 in) long and has to have a number of buds. The sets are taken from older trees and are pushed into the ground, 30 cm (12 in) apart, in rows 60 cm (24 in) from each other, so that the weeding, so necessary for a good healthy crop, can take place. There may be as many as 17 000 sets to an acre (0·4 hectares). Stock collected and planted during the winter will be ready for growth in the following spring. Roots develop beneath the soil and sap will rise, allowing the aerial buds to grow.

Apart from weed control, the crop does not need a great deal of attention. Willows are deciduous and the leaves which fall in the autumn decay and provide a valuable source of humus for next year's growth. The young willows grow for between 2 and 3 years; they are pruned at the end of the first year's growth to encourage the production of strong roots and by the end of the third year, the stems are long enough for basketry. Osier beds provide plenty

Once osiers have become established, they can be used for many years. The rods are cut regularly from stools which may have been in use for up to 50 years.

of material for many years; the 'stools' increase in size annually and the young stems may be harvested every 3 years.

Hybridisation, both planned and accidental, has produced as many as seventy varieties, e.g. the golden, black, Dutch, Spanish, champion and stone osier. All are now used for basket-making. The Welsh osier is used for fish and eel traps, because the wood has a bitter taste, which the fish do not like; once inside the trap, the fish do not bite their way out—or so the marsh man believed. Other species of osier have more universal uses in craftwork.

Once cut, most rods are used as they are, a condition called *in the round*. Others may be split and these are known as *skeins*. The high grade stems are used in basket-making, but the rougher material is reserved for the construction of hurdles.

The willow is cut in the winter when the sap has gone down. Using a hook, the cutter employs an upward movement, making his incision as close as possible to the stool. The stems, stacked in heaps, are then arranged in bundles, a piece of osier being used to secure them; bundles for sale have a standard diameter of 37 in (94 cm) at the base.

Green rods are used for making cheap hurdles and are not treated before being made up. *Brown rods* are derived either from steamed green rods or from better quality green rods left in the open air to dry naturally. Brown rods get their colour when dried in the atmosphere or steamed. Soaking may be necessary before use to make them pliable. They are used mainly for garden furniture and rough baskets. Good quality green rods are boiled for up to 5 hours, during which time the tannin soaks into the wood, producing the buff colour. They are stored while still damp and are stripped later.

Willow rods can be used for a variety of purposes. Here they are being made into a basket.

Originally made for dividing up areas of land, hurdles are now used mainly for decorative purposes in gardens.

The best quality are the carefully selected *white rods* which are stored in water, either in tanks or in specially constructed pits, from winter through to May, when the buds will be open and the sap has started to rise. The stems are passed through an iron device called a *brake* which grips the bark as the wood passes through and strips it off, revealing the white rod. Norfolk basket-makers used to employ women to do this for the princely sum of $2\frac{1}{2}d$ (1n.p.) per complete bundle.

Willow has been used for making a variety of articles in the past—bullock feeding-baskets, bushel skeps, fish baskets, potato baskets, fruit baskets and linen baskets—but plastic and wire have largely replaced it. Today ornamental dog baskets and log baskets, as well as garden furniture and hurdles, keep many craftsmen busy.

RUSH-WEAVING

Man soon realised that rushes were particularly durable and, even before he learned how to weave them into mats, he scattered them on the floors of his homes, to provide a cheap covering which could be replaced once it was worn. He also dipped rushes into fat so that, when lit, they acted as a primitive candle. Rush-weaving became an established craft in the Middle Ages when rushes were used to make carpets, mats, and baskets.

The Gladden Cutters Return *by P. H. Emerson.*

Both the bulrush (*Schoenoplectus lacustris*), known as *bolder*, and the lesser reed-mace (*Typha angustifolia*), known as *gladden*, were employed, each having its particular uses. Bolder was made into rush-matting, but because of its scarcity, little home-produced material is now used, although some is imported.

Gladden was used in the weaving of a type of basket known as a *frail*, although a mixture of this and bolder was also used. It was also made into horse collars as it was easy on the neck, and these were popular in East Anglia. Industries grew up where there was a plentiful supply of materials, such as the River Deben in Suffolk, where the Deben rush-weavers, whose headquarters were at Debenham, originated. However, the supply has now disappeared and material is brought in from Bedfordshire and Northamptonshire. To ensure that the rushes meet their stringent requirements, the rush-cutting is arranged by the weavers.

Difficulty has always been experienced in harvesting the rush, because its roots are under the water. Using a typical reaping hook, and working in water, a good cutter can harvest as many as 100 bundles in a day. As the rushes are cut, they are laid on the water and are later collected and bundled together. The bundles are formed into a raft which floats down the waterway to a suitable collecting point. Once removed from the water, the rushes are allowed to drain on the bank before being taken away.

Heat cannot be used in the drying process as this would make the rushes brittle and useless, so they have to dry naturally. Quality varies, even within one area, and both stiff and pliable stems can be found. The pliable stems are used for hand-weaving, e.g. for hats, baskets and table mats, while the stiff stems, being more resilient, are used for chair seats and on looms to make rush-matting.

Eel-catching

IN DAYS GONE BY, the marshland provided valuable supplies of food. Many animals living in the marsh, such as eels and ducks, were caught, using methods which had obviously been handed down from one generation to another.

Eels, which are a valuable food source, have been caught in marshland areas for hundreds of years and, in this time, a variety of methods have been used. In one such method, known as *babbing*, a number of earthworms were threaded through with a needle, to which was attached some worsted or wool thread. The worms were then tied together in a bunch and then fastened to a stick, usually of hazel.

With this bait, the eel-catcher would set out, preferably on a warm summer evening when the river was low. A worm, held in the water, would be grabbed by an eel which would hold on to it. The eel-catcher would then lift his stick out of the water, complete with worms and drop the eel into a bath, either on the bank, or in a boat if he was working on the water.

Spearing, now illegal, was also used for catching eels. An eel-pick—alternatively called a *glave* or *gleeve*—consisted of 4–6 flat, usually barbed, blades, attached to a head. The pick was fixed to a 3 m (9 ft) pole. The eel-catcher would thrust his glave into the bottom mud where he hoped eels would be. As the technique was passed from father to son, marshmen were adept at using these implements. Narrow-bladed fish darts were used in a similar fashion to catch other fish, including pike.

A third method involved the use of eel-traps. These were long baskets, preferably made from Welsh osiers, and had backward-pointing rods arranged along the inside, so that eels could wriggle their way into the trap but not out

Pulling up the eel nets.

Once collected and emptied from the net, the eels are stored in the eel trunk which is then submerged in water. Eels will probably be added to the 'catch' for several days until there are enough to sell.

again. A suitable plug was placed in the other end. The traps were more effective if bait, such as the entrails of rabbits or decayed fish, was used. The eel-catcher would check his traps each morning, tipping his catch into an *eel trunk*. This was a large box, with a lid and small holes drilled in the side for water to circulate. The eels could be kept in this store for several weeks, without any visible signs of deterioration. Fresh catches would be added daily, until there was enough to be either collected or sent to market. Nowadays, eels are still caught, collected in tankers and transported by ferry from Felixstowe to Denmark, where they sell for high prices. Smaller ones are sent to the London market where they are cooked and sold as jellied eels.

The fourth method of catching eels is by using *eel setts*. These are nets placed across a river or dyke. With wings attached, they are fashioned with a *belly* which ends in a *pod*. To enable the bottom to sink, the net is weighted down with chain and there are corks on the top to enable this section to float. By fixing the nets in a certain way, it is possible to raise and lower them. At night lights are lit on each side of the dyke and further warnings that an eel sett is in operation are given by warning signs and red flags. This is essential, because the nets are expensive and could easily be damaged by boats navigating the stretch of river or dyke where the eel sett is positioned.

This method of eel-catching is an old and well-tried one. As long ago as 1576, there were no fewer than thirty-eight licenced eel setts on rivers in Broadland—the Bure, Yare and Waveney. In those times, the nets were placed in position on moonless nights and proved very productive. As many as 700 kg (110 stone) were recorded as being taken on the Bure in one evening and 2100 kg (330 stone) on the Yare. Although the catches are much smaller now, the system is still used.

The *Fyke net* method uses a net in a different way. Instead of being set

This net is known as a 'Fyke net'. Hoops positioned at regular intervals keep the net open. Eels then have free access and ultimately end up in the pod, from which they cannot escape.

across the dyke, the net is set along it. This method is also used in lakes and on the Broads. The net is made from lengths of netting, with tunnels at intervals, each leading to a pod. The pods are kept open by metal hoops. It is not uncommon for several nets to be placed in position, end to end, thus covering several hundreds of metres of the dyke or open water. When the eels swim up against the net, they turn at right-angles and then find themselves in the pod. As the netting is reversed here they are unable to make their escape. This and the eel sett method are adopted wherever eel-catching is on a commercial scale as it provides large catches. The Fyke method is used especially in the summer months.

Wild-fowling

AT SOME POINT IN HIS HISTORY, man became a hunter and, undoubtedly, certain areas proved more profitable than others. The marshland region, despite its lack of any really suitable mammals, was rich in wild fowl. Although wild-fowling has acquired a sporting reputation in the second half of the twentieth century, in the past, wild-fowlers made a living from killing and selling birds, which were an important food resource.

At that time, the marshland covered a much larger area, and wild-fowling was much more widespread. Large stretches of water were shrouded by vast reed-beds, which were a veritable treasure house for the wild fowl seeking food and for the wild-fowler seeking his catch. With little else from which to earn a living, the people living in the marshland made as much use as possible not only of the wild fowl, but of the fish and plants as well.

It is difficult to imagine the land in those days, but in Saxon England life in marshland areas must have been very unpleasant. Houses would have been built where there were outcrops—perhaps of gravel, or where the land had built up due to deposition. The whole area was damp and unhealthy, with numerous insects, including mosquitoes, and, as a result many people died 'before their time'. Travelling was difficult, since much of the terrain, if not covered with water, was very boggy. Getting from place to place was originally achieved by boat, although causeways were eventually built. Some causeways were on stilts, others were merely plank walkways. The local people, however, had no exclusive rights to the wild fowl. Many species, such as herons, cranes, swans and bitterns, were reserved for the King or Queen and the abbeys, which were established in various places, were charged with providing these birds for royal banquets.

Killing birds for food gradually became an accomplished art. For example, James I, during his reign, organised hawking excursions in fenland Britain. The art of falconry developed, in which hawks and falcons were used to capture such delicacies as teal, mallard, herons and geese.

The local people became very familiar with the wildlife of the marsh and gradually evolved more successful ways of hunting and trapping. They used snares and nets, as well as bird-lime.

Although there were laws, even in mediaeval times, which covered the sale of livestock from marsh and fen, the local people devised their own marketing system and considered it their right to sell the eggs of water birds, such as teal, moorhens and a variety of other ducks. Partly-domesticated wild fowl, e.g. geese and swans, were kept in and around the houses. When fattened, they were rounded up, driven onto the water and taken to market.

Life was difficult and it is no wonder that the marshland dweller was a very hardy character. Those who made their living from the marsh, often did so from a combination of fishing and fowling. Others found that casual wild-fowling provided a part-time although somewhat hazardous job. As well as obtaining a free supply of meat from the birds which they caught, the fowlers made money by selling any surplus.

Wild fowl, which once were able to escape their captors, fared less well once guns and gunpowder arrived in the marshes. Two types of gun came

Gunner Working Up To Fowl *by P. H. Emerson, from* Life and Landscape in the
Norfolk Broads, *1886.*

into common use: the shoulder gun and the punt gun. The punt gun, which
was much the larger, was, as the name suggests, fired from a marshland boat
or sometimes from dyke banks. With the arrival of the punt gun, the stocks of
wild fowl decreased. Instead of killing single birds, as with the shoulder-held
gun, the punt gun, rather like a miniature cannon, had a far more dramatic
impact. When fired into sizeable flocks of swimming ducks, each volley
quickly added to the wild-fowler's bag. The size of the day's haul can be best
understood by looking at the records for a day's punt-gunning. In 1860, a
party of thirty-two punt-gunners on the Blackwater Estuary in Essex caused
the death of 954 Brent geese.

Although lucrative, wild-fowling was tough; much of the work took place
in icy conditions in the colder months of the year. The men used to smother
their bare chests with goose grease, which they then covered with brown
paper before putting on their clothes. It took a lot of effort and a lot of grease,
and it was just as troublesome to get the grease off again, so the wild-fowlers
often kept the fat on their chests for a week at a time, sleeping with it!

The punts which the wild-fowler used were 4·9-6·0 m (16–20 ft) long,
clinker-built and without decking. Camouflage was essential and a variety of
marshland vegetation, including sedge and reed, was draped over the bow.
At night, when the ducks were resting, the punt was manoeuvred silently
through the water. Two small paddles were used to propel the boat and the
punt-man worked these while lying flat on the bottom of the boat. His punt
gun, 2 m (6·5 ft) long and with 2·5-5 cm (1–2 in) bore, would be put into
position with the minimum amount protruding over the bow of the boat.

With a group of resting birds in sight, the punt-man would hit the boat

25

This is the pipe of a duck decoy. Food which is placed inside the pipe draws in the ducks. They are then attracted by a small dog, especially trained to lure the ducks further into the decoy. He will appear and then disappear behind reed screens along the side of the pipe.

to make the birds rise a little from the water and then fire low across the water to ensure a bigger bag. As shot splayed out across the water, the resounding boom would scatter the wildfowl over a considerable distance. His effort would probably net him about twenty or so ducks. It would be some time before groups of birds returned to the water, so that there would be only half a dozen or so chances to shoot during each evening's work.

In winter, when the marshland water became frozen, the punt-gunner used different tactics. He mounted his punt on a sledge so that it would move easily across the frozen surface. He abandoned his oars and replaced them with either knives or ice picks, to propel his boat forward.

Punt-gunning is still practised in many parts of the country but to a far lesser extent than in the past, and for sport rather than necessity.

The decoy is perhaps the most interesting 'invention' of the marsh-dwellers. There are two kinds. The true decoy consists of a long, usually curved, tube of netting, known as a *pipe*, leading to a quiet secluded pond. There are usually several of these pipes. Wild ducks are attracted to the pond, either by baiting or by tamed wild ducks specially reared for this purpose. The ducks are free to come and go and to feed on the marsh.

Once the ducks are established on the pond, the decoy man can begin to entice them into the pipes. This is achieved either by baiting or by using a specially trained dog known as a *piper*. The dog runs alongside the pipe behind a reed screen. Gaps in the screen make it seem to appear and disappear and this attracts the ducks into the pipe in an attempt to follow the dog. The ducks are thus led along the pipe which gets progressively narrower and eventually ends in a keep net where the ducks are trapped. The ducks can thus be caught without disturbing the others still on the pond. Such a decoy can be used for some time, as new birds are constantly being attracted to the pond. Such decoys are still in use to catch birds for ringing purposes. In earlier times, the first ducks were usually taken in the colder months when they could fetch a high price as fresh meat.

The other type of decoy is more primitive and consists of a funnel-shaped enclosure over water. When ducks are moulting they are unable to fly and so are a prime target for the activities of the punt-men. The men in their boats surround the flocks of flightless birds and drive them into the enclosures, where they are killed. Flight nets are used for birds such as plovers.

In the past, the species which were shot included a variety of duck, as well as geese, coot, moorhen, golden plover, woodcock, curlew, snipe, wood pigeon and pheasant. Even the less commonly encountered birds were not safe from the wild-fowlers. Not only would birds suitable for eating be taken, but there was, at one time, a good trade in interesting species for taxidermists. These were used as 'ornaments' in the home. Nowadays, the variety of species caught is much less, due, in no small measure, to the reduction in wild fowl numbers. This is a result of drainage and over-shooting in the past, among other factors. The principal ducks taken now are mallard, teal and wigeon— in that order. Woodcock, snipe and pheasant, along with some wild geese and also rabbits and hares, make up the rest of the bag.

Five methods are currently used in modern fowling. In rough walking up, the hunters walk across the grazing marshes or along the marsh walls. Species taken in these walks include a few duck, some snipe and pigeon, as well as pheasant, hare and rabbit.

Occasionally there are organised drives in which groups of wild-fowlers move across the grazing marshes. The most likely victims here are duck, snipe, pheasant and hare.

In flighting, a flight pond is used, which may be either natural or artificial, and shallow enough for a variety of water plants to become established; this is an essential pre-requisite. To entice geese and ducks, food is introduced, usually large amounts of barley, although other grain is used. Various duck and goose species will come in at dusk to take their fill, providing an easy target. Shoots take place about once a fortnight. In a variation of this method, wild-fowlers will shoot ducks which visit corn stubble where grain, dropped by the combine, provides food.

In winter, wigeon, often in large flocks, come to feed on the grazing levels and they are driven up, or flighted, from hides made from bales of straw or from the gateways over the marshland dykes. This is not a particularly effective method and only small numbers are shot in this way.

In some of the marsh carrs, organised game shoots take place and the birds are sent up by beaters and driven over the guns.

Conservation of wild fowl is one of the aims of certain groups, which rear ducks especially for shooting, rather than depleting the numbers in the wild. For this purpose, small flight ponds are excavated in marshland areas. Here ducks are reared and released. Over the years, this method has become increasingly popular and most wild-fowling clubs affiliated to WAGBI (the Wild-fowlers' Association of Great Britain and Ireland now the British Association for Shooting and Conservation) have the rearing and release of ducks into the wild as part of their policy.

Marshland boats

THERE ARE A NUMBER OF CRAFT which have been developed specifically for navigation on marshland areas. Some, like the wherry, are specifically associated with certain parts of the country. Others are found in many different areas.

The *wherry*, fine at the waterline and rounded on the deck, was a heavy vessel. Keel, stern and sternpost, as well as the frame, were made of oak. However, in spite of its bulk, it could sail in shallow waters, even when fully loaded. The massive mast was made from larch or pitch pine and was fitted to a tabernacle. It was counterbalanced by cast iron and lead weights, weighing up to 1780 kg (3920 lb), so that it could be lowered for negotiating bridges. The sail, made up of more than 100 m² (120 yd²) of canvas, was traditionally black, coloured by mixing coal tar, herring oil and lamp black, which strengthened and preserved the material.

Wherries plied the rivers of the Norfolk and Suffolk Broadland, carrying every conceivable cargo. Today the *Albion*, owned by the Norfolk Wherry Trust, is the only surviving craft.

Punts were also used and were of two types. The *marsh punt*, used deep in the marshland, was rather narrow and light in weight. Low in profile, it was clinker-built and generally about 4·8 m (16 ft) long. A movable plank served as the seat. Two means of propulsion were used: oars and a flat-capped punting pole, known in East Anglia as a *quant*. The quant was made from larch and was between 3 and 3·5 m (10 and 12 ft) long. Punts were useful craft on the

This is the wherry Albion, *the last of the trading wherries which, at one time, were seen regularly on the Broads. This craft has been restored and is preserved by the Norfolk Wherry Trust. It is in operation and can be seen on the Norfolk Broads.*

*The marsh punt is an all-purpose boat,
capable of floating in very shallow waters.
It is propelled by a* quant, *a long pole
which is pushed down into the mud.*

*Reed-lighters are used to transport reeds along the marshland waterways. Here a craft is
being loaded. They were useful for carrying other marsh material, including hay and
sedge.*

river and, if painted with tar, they were very durable. They were used for transporting small amounts of marshland vegetation, such as sedges, reeds and rushes, and also as more general marshland runabouts.

Although ordinary marsh punts were used for wild-fowling in marshland areas, a variation, the *gun punt*, was used in more open areas of water, such as the lakes and Broads, as well as around the coast. The gun punt was very narrow and double-ended, with a low beam. Decking was a feature fore and aft, as well as on the sides. On average, the punt was about 5·5 m (18 ft) long and the gun was mounted forward. It was propelled by short oars or a quant, but a paddle was used as the boat approached groups of wild fowl resting on the water.

The *reed-lighter* is a completely open craft, with no seating and is used for carrying reeds. There are three kinds: half, three-quarters and full load lighters. A full load lighter has a 2·5 m (8·5 ft) beam and an average length of 7·6 m (25·5 ft). It can be manoeuvred either with a quant or with oars. A full lighter is capable of carrying two cartloads of reeds; the others can carry proportional quantities.

PART II
MARSHLAND VEGETATION
Plants

THE MARSHLAND FLORA owes its rich and varied nature to the amounts of
dissolved minerals which occur in the marshland soil. The other distinctive
feature of the marshland habitat, whether it is a small area around a lake, or a
much larger expanse, is the zonation of plant species which results in a variety
of plant communities. Rich and fertile marshland areas are often drained and,
where this happens, many of the once common plants have either become
very much rarer or have disappeared altogether. In addition to those marshes
which occur as narrow fringes around lakes, others have been formed where
regular flooding takes place.

The plants which grow in places where it is merely damp do not seem to
have the same problems to overcome as those which inhabit waterlogged
soils, where oxygen, which does not dissolve easily in water, is at a premium.
The plants, however, have evolved techniques for dealing with this situation.
In some species, such as the purple loosestrife there are distinct spongy swellings of tissue and, because of the spaces between the cells, diffusion of gases
can take place.

All habitats are dynamic and ever-changing and alders, where they have
become established, eventually turn the area into alder carr. Silting takes
place around the roots of various plants, including trees, and this effectively
raises the level of the land, so that waterlogging is eventually eliminated.

The plants which occur in the marshland habitat can be grouped according to the zone which they occupy. One group, which includes the familiar
duckweeds, consists of free-floating plants and its distribution depends on
the amount of open water available. Such plants can be found on almost any
water surface because they are not affected by depth. There are also many
free-floating microscopic species, such as the diatoms and desmids, which
occur within a metre or so of the surface.

A second group consists of completely submerged plants, like the Canadian pondweed, which root in the bottom mud. These typical water plants
are correctly termed *hydrophytes*. They are fully adapted for an aquatic existence and are incapable of life on land because, among other things, they lack
supporting tissue and the ability to absorb oxygen and carbon dioxide from
the air. They can be found wherever sufficient light can penetrate the water.

There are also a number of plant species which, although rooted in the
bottom mud, have a stem which reaches to the surface of the water and bears
a variety of leaves, both submerged and floating. This group includes the
water lilies and crowfoots. Their distribution is limited by depth.

On the water's edge can be found the emergent plants—the swamp species.
These have their roots in shallow water but most of the plant is above the
surface. One undeniably typical species of this area is the reed and hence this
area is often referred to as *reed-swamp*. The leaves of this plant form dense
cover and its rhizomes bind and hold the sediments carried by flood waters.

If unchecked, the reed encroaches on the water, eventually turning the whole area into reed-swamp as mud accumulates around its roots. Where the reed does not take over completely, other species may occur, particularly rushes, the branched bur-reed, the reed-mace, bulrush or common club rush, flote grass, sweet reed-grass and sweet flag.

The willow herbs are known colonisers of a variety of habitats and one species in particular, the great hairy willow-herb may become established in the reed-swamp. Because of the rapid growth of plants in this area, the amount of humus returned to the soil annually is very high, producing nutrient-rich soils. It is not surprising, therefore, that drainage, although expensive, has been practiced in order to yield vast tracts of very fertile land.

As soil accumulates, the area rises slightly with a change from reed-swamp to marsh conditions. Although the soil surface is visible, which is not the case in the zones already described, the water level is only just below it and marsh soils are waterlogged. Flooding is a frequent occurrence and can be especially dramatic after heavy rainfall.

Many of the plants in the marsh region exhibit luxurious growth. Water loss is no problem, because there is generally an abundant supply of water, but large air spaces within the plant are necessary because air is not always readily available in the waterlogged soil.

Where large tussocks of sedge grow, sediments collect around them and, ultimately, the weight becomes so great that whole plants sink into the wet substrate. In this way, small pools are created and open-water species are likely to colonise these.

Decay begins once the sedges have become buried and the formation of peat inevitably follows. Some tree species capable of withstanding damp conditions may begin to germinate, including the alder and the willows. The haphazard sinking of the sedge tussocks results in an unstable substrate and trees do not grow well. They are unevenly distributed and growth is far from regular. Their establishment, however, marks a change in the character of the habitat and, as more soil is deposited, together with colonisation by other species, a more stable situation arises.

As this happens, larger trees are able to establish themselves and thus the gradual change from reed-swamp to carr takes place. In this marsh woodland habitat, the alder becomes the dominant tree, although other species, including birch gain a foothold. This is the typical climax vegetation, known as *alder carr*.

Variations occur from region to region, but the ultimate and final stage in marshland vegetation, if it is allowed to develop is alder carr, where, apart from the main trees, other herbaceous plants will be encountered.

It has to be remembered that man has influenced the marshland flora for a very long time. Although his early ancestors had not learned the art of draining the marsh, nevertheless they did mow areas, using the vegetation for feeding their livestock and the reed for thatching. In drier areas, they brought in their stock to feed on the plants. As wild animals invade the area, they also alter the vegetation cover. Grazing animals, like the rabbit, tend to keep out taller species in favour of shorter herbs.

Where conditions become favourable, gaps which appear among the reeds will give tree seedlings a chance to become established. Once this process has begun, the vegetation will develop eventually, through scrub, which consists of alders and sallows intermingled with a number of bush-like species, such as guelder rose and the buckthorns, to woodland.

The level of the area gradually rises, a process which normally takes hundreds of years, until, relatively speaking, the water table is lowered and tree species usually associated with woodland habitats can become established.

Characteristic plants of still quiet waters, the duckweeds (*Lemna* spp.) will colonise large expanses of water in favourable conditions. Duckweeds are small floating plants, consisting of a leaf-like thallus which has one or more root-like filaments, or *rhizoids*, on the underside. These extract nutrients from the water. They reproduce mainly by budding. The flowers, although generally inconspicuous and rare, are either male or female. Female flowers have a single pistil and the male ones have a single anther.

The most widespread is the lesser duckweed *Lemna minor*. The thallus is either egg-shaped or round and, in this species, is seldom more than 2–3 mm (0·08–0·12 in) in diameter. There is a single filament growing out from the undersurface. In contrast, the great duckweed (*Lemna polyrrhiza*) produces many roots from the underside of the thallus, which has a decidedly reddish tinge. The gibbous duckweed (*Lemna gibba*) may be as much as 5 mm (0·2 in) in diameter, with a round thallus which has only one root. In winter, duckweeds sink to the bottom where the warmer water protects them during adverse conditions.

The fairy moss (*Azolla filiculoides*), a native of North America, occurs mainly in southern Britain and various parts of Europe. Beneath the oval-shaped branching leaflets of this floating species, there are rhizoids which extract the plant's mineral requirements from the water. It is a fern and so produces spores, which are contained in a spherical sporangium. They are liberated when the sporangium bursts.

The greater bladderwort or common bladderwort (*Utricularia vulgaris*) gets its name from the small bladders on its leaves. Inwardly pointing hairs on the bladders allow small water insects to enter, but prevent their escape and, over a period of time, the insects decay, releasing mineral salts which the plant absorbs and uses for food. The air-filled bladders also help to support the plant in the water. The plant is not particularly common. The yellow flowers appear from July to August and are barely noticeable. With the arrival of autumn, the plant produces small buds which, because they are filled with stored food, are heavy and sink to the bottom. They remain there until the following spring, when they begin to germinate.

Found in still or slow-flowing water, the whorled water milfoil (*Myrio-phyllum verticillatum*) is anchored to the substrate by its stem and, with the exception of the flowering spike, the rest of the plant remains submerged. Flowering from June to August, the small blossoms are well adapted for pollination by the wind. Pollen from the taller male flowers falls onto the female ones.

As well as seeds, water milfoil also produces winter buds, either at the end

Water soldier inhabits still and slow-flowing waters. Where it becomes well established it covers large areas. In deep water, the plant may be completely submerged. In shallower water, it is semi-submerged with floating leaves.

of the shoots or inside the leaf axils. They pass the winter in the mud at the bottom of the water while the rest of the plant dies.

A number of species of the perennial *Potamogeton* water plants grow in the waters of marshy areas. Identification is a problem because they vary so much in form, depending on the depth and type of water in which they grow. Easy hybridisation does not help matters.

Potamogetons usually grow in clumps, which may spread outwards for 100–200 cm (39–78 in). The flowers, which are very small, do not have petals.

The water soldier (*Stratiotes aloides*) sinks to the bottom of the pond after it has flowered and produced seeds and rises again in early summer. Once actively growing, the partly submerged plant floats easily. The saw-edged, spiny leaves form rosettes, each leaf growing up to 40 cm (15·5 in). The roots obtain nutrients either from the water or from the substrate.

The buds, which develop in the axils, grow into runners from which new plants will grow when they root. This is important because the seeds which are produced do not mature. In July and August, individual plants bear either male or female flowers, the former being much rarer than the latter. The plant is disappearing in some areas, such as East Anglia, where it is now considered uncommon in certain places.

The floating frogbit (*Hydrocharis morsus-ranae*) is common in many watery areas including ponds and ditches. It is not rooted in mud but has aquatic roots which absorb the plant's requirements from the water. Floating leaves, up to 4 cm (1·5 in) in diameter, grow out from the roots. They are round in outline, with a heart-shaped base, and form a rosette on the water surface. Stolons are produced during the growing season, so that, when growth ceases towards the end of summer, the plant covers a large area. Winter buds, which are produced at the extremities of the last stolons to be formed, are heavy with starch and sink once they have broken away from the parent plant. They become lighter when growth begins in spring and drift to the water surface where growth continues.

Each flower is either male or female and, in some places, only one kind is produced, so that fertilisation cannot occur and no seeds are formed.

Although the water starworts (*Callitriche* spp.) are widely distributed, even occurring in small pools which dry up in hot weather, they are intolerant of pollution. Starworts have both floating and submerged leaves. Distinguishing between the four species of starworts is usually only possible when fruits appear in the autumn. In the British Isles, *Callitriche stagnalis* is probably the most common species, whereas *C.platycarpa* is the most common in central Europe.

C. stagnalis grows equally well on mud and in both slow-flowing and still water. Separate male and female flowers appear; the latter are the larger. The fruits are broad and winged.

The arrowhead (*Sagittaria sagittifolia*) is well adapted to the aquatic environment. Rooted in the bottom mud of slow-moving lowland rivers, the creeping stems throw up three types of leaves. Those above the water are arrow-shaped, hence the plant's name. The leaves that float on the water are broad and the submerged leaves are narrow and grass-like. The single-sexed flowers which appear from May to September are borne on the same stem, which rises well above the leaves. The smaller male flowers occur towards the top of the stem and the female ones occur further down.

The amphibious bistort (*Polygonum amphibium*) has two distinct forms, depending on its situation. The terrestrial form has slightly hairy leaves and stems, in contrast to the smooth leaves of the aquatic form. In the latter, the leaves are often heart-shaped and the long stalks enable them to float on the surface. The land-living form has shorter stalks and the leaves are held upright. The pink flowers are open from July to September.

Two species of water lilies occur in marshland areas. The yellow water lily (*Nuphar lutea*) is the commonest as it can colonise many different types of water, including relatively swift-flowing rivers. Indeed, once its rootstock has become established it is difficult to eradicate, often causing problems in navigable water.

The floating wide leathery leaves have veins parallel to the mid-vein. The first leaves develop near the tip of the rhizome and are thin and cabbage-like. Under normal conditions, the more familiar floating leaves then grow, but in unfavourable conditions only submerged leaves may be found. The triangular stems, because they contain air-filled spaces, help the leaves to float.

The large rhizome may grow to a length of 300 cm (118 in) and from it numerous adventitious roots emerge. Solitary flowers borne on long stalks appear from June to August and are held a few centimetres above the water. The black seeds, which are enclosed in a jelly-like substance, develop inside a poppy-like capsule from which they are eventually released.

The much less common white water lily (*Nymphaea alba*) is more attractive and was called the water rose in the Middle Ages. It inhabits still water where the rhizome never exceeds 100 cm (39 in) in length.

The large leathery leaves are glossy on the upper surface with a purplish tinge underneath and float on the water. They may completely cover an area, blocking out the light and preventing other species from growing. The rounded leaf stalk may be as much as 300 cm (118 in) long. The plant is in flower from June to August; each bloom is 9–12 cm (3·5–4·7 in) in diameter and is made up of spirally-arranged white petals.

The fruits are enclosed in structures described as *brandy bottles*. They float at first but eventually become submerged, whereupon they burst open, releasing numerous pink seeds.

The Canadian pondweed (*Elodea canadensis*) was brought to Europe from North America in the 1850s. It rapidly colonised the areas into which it was introduced, causing many problems to boats on the rivers and canals. However, it seems to have found its level and, generally, is not now considered a nuisance. In fact, in many waterways, it is valued for its oxygenating properties, which benefit other plants and animals.

In Europe it bears only female flowers and so seeds are not produced. This is not a problem, however, because small pieces break off to form new plants. Winter buds appear in autumn and these give rise to new plants in the following spring. The rounded leaves have a delicate toothed margin.

Characteristically, the flote grass (*Glyceria fluitans*) inhabits areas of either slow-flowing or stagnant water. The flat leaves, up to 8 mm (0·3 in) wide, are very weak and where they do not actually float on the water surface, they tend to bend towards it. The leaves and stem of this perennial species rise from a creeping rhizome to a height of between 40 and 120 cm (16–47 in). From the flowering spikes, which are up to 50 cm (20 in) high, smaller spikelets of 2–3 cm (0·8–1·2 in) arise, carrying between seven and eleven flowers, which appear from June to September. The fruits which develop are no more than 3 mm (0·12 in) long and float away to form new plants.

Where seeds were collected in the past, presumably because of their nutritional value, they were referred to as *manna groats*.

The water crowfoots (*Ranunculus* spp.), which belong to the buttercup family, are not easy to distinguish between, as thirteen species grow in water. Below the surface, the much dissected thread-like leaves bear little resemblance to the floating leaves. The latter, kidney-shaped with a glossy upper surface, are scalloped along the edges. There are also many leaf shapes intermediate to those of the submerged and floating leaves.

The reed (*Phragmites australis*) is undoubtedly the most valuable commercial marshland plant. Although more widespread in lowland areas, it occurs over the whole of the British Isles. It is a particularly conspicuous species and is Britain's largest native grass. It forms large stands in marshes and also grows in shallow water at the edges of lakes, ditches and dykes.

The tough, grass-like, smooth grey-green leaves are 20–60 cm (8–24 in) long. The entire plant reaches a height of 150–300 cm (59–118 in) and is spread by means of extensive stout creeping rhizomes and stolons. These are valuable because they help to stabilise mud.

The plume-like flowers droop on the stems from late August until October. Dark before they open, they become a purplish brown and more loosely arranged when they unfold. The silky hairs give the flower head a more greyish colour, whilst still retaining some of the purple. Once ripe, the light seeds are carried by the wind. The leaves fall off the plant in autumn, leaving the stems bare; these are harvested for thatching (p. 8).

The sweet flag (*Acorus calamus*) establishes itself around the shallow water

The white water lily is seldom found in water deeper than 1·5 m (59 in). The rhizome sends up long-stalked floating leaves. Other leaves below the surface resemble those of cultivated cabbages. The first flowers appear in June.

The reed is one of the few marshland plants which has any commercial value. Where the rhizomes become well established they spread over large areas, giving rise to extensive stands. The flower head is typically known as feather among thatchers. The flower heads, green at first, darken to brown, sometimes with a purple tinge, as they age.

Favouring muddy situations, the bur-reed occurs around the margins of ponds and lakes and is often associated with reed and reed-mace. The underground rhizome produces many emergent leaves and gives rise to large clumps of the plants.

The great water dock has typical dock-like leaves, although these are much larger than in the terrestrial forms. Lance-shaped in outline, the lower ones are the largest.

margins of marshy areas. It is a perennial and a member of the arum family.

It was brought from southern Asia to the British Isles in the sixteenth century and is now established over much of Britain, except the north. The numerous inconspicuous green flowers which make up the inflorescence never become fertilised in Britain. Propagation occurs when pieces of the underground rhizome break off. The leaves are sword-like with crinkly edges and, when crushed, give off a pleasant vanilla-like aroma. This characteristic made them popular on the floors of houses and churches in earlier times when they used to be mixed with rushes. The bitter rhizomes were used to cure swellings of the gums, anaemia, liver and intestinal disorders and to relieve gout.

Colonising the fringes of lowland lakes and other freshwater areas, the perennial reed-grass or great water grass (*Glyceria maxima*) reaches a height of about 200 cm (79 in). It is a true grass and where conditions are favourable it will produce lush cover, spreading by means of underground rhizomes from which erect stems arise.

A spike 20–40 cm (8–16 in) high bears the flowers between July and August. Many spikelets arise from this, each of which bears between five and eight flowers. At first the tips of the flowers are light green, but they change to either brown or purple as they ripen.

The great water dock (*Rumex hydrolaphatum*) has large leaves. The slightly branched form of this perennial species may reach a maximum height of about 200 cm (79 in). The broad, lance-shaped leaves are typically dock-shaped and those nearest the water reach a maximum height of 100 cm (39 in). The plant produces flowers from June through to August.

A localised and very poisonous plant, the cowbane (*Cicuta virosa*) occurs in eastern Scotland, northern Ireland and East Anglia, where it grows in shallow water, in amongst other aquatic plants. The rhizome from which the plant develops is divided into a number of small hollow chambers. Stems which grow from this reach a height of between 100 and 150 cm (39 and 59 in) with a number of slender ridges along its length. The flowers are borne on umbels in July and August.

Also known as marshwort, the fool's watercress (*Apium nodiflorum*) belongs to the same family as the dropworts. With its mixture of upright and creeping stems, this hairless perennial varies from 30–90 cm (12–36 in) in height. Although it is an umbellifer, it differs from other members of this group, because the flowers are either borne on small stalks or are stalkless.

It flowers from July to September in shallow ponds and ditches and by the sides of streams, which it colonises. West Country folk used to collect the plant and cook and serve it with meat dishes.

Despite its name, the water violet (*Hottonia palustris*) is not related to the violets, but is a member of the primrose family. Particularly common in the eastern part of the British Isles, the plant grows in ditches and pools, flourishing where light is plentiful.

Although typically aquatic, with leaves growing under the water surface, it occasionally grows on land, in which case it does not flower. Because the leaves are dissected, they are less prone to damage by the water. Flowers with pale pink or lilac petals are borne on leafless stems in May and June. Once fertilised, the seeds develop inside a capsule-like fruit. When this opens, there are five slits through which the seeds escape.

Propagation also occurs when pieces of branches are broken off and carried away in the water. Those which are dropped in suitable places may germinate. Stolon-like branches produce winter buds in autumn which survive adverse conditions and begin to grow in the following spring.

The branched bur-reed (*Sparganium erectum*) has a globe-like flower head, made up of numerous very small single-sexed flowers. Strategically placed for wind pollination, the female flowers are below the male ones. After fertilisation, bur-like seeds develop, the feature from which the plant gets its name. These provide wild-fowl with a supply of food in autumn and winter.

Growing in either running or stagnant water or in marshes, large numbers of branched bur-reeds may cover substantial areas. Their dense clumps provide not only nesting sites but also roosting places for some water fowl.

A relative of the arrowhead (p. 34), the water plantain (*Alisma plantago-aquatica*) grows in amongst other emergent vegetation in marshy areas and in the mud of bays, in lakes and in ditches. The ribbon-like aquatic leaves are produced first, followed by the plantain-like emergent leaves. The stem may be up to 100 cm (39 in) high, with many white or reddish white three-petalled flowers. These only open in the afternoon and can be seen from June to September.

Found in shallow water, the bogbean (*Menyanthes trifoliata*) is a relative of the gentians. Stems arise from an underwater creeping rhizome. They float if in deep water or creep along in shallower conditions. The first flowers appear in May and June in lowland areas and much later in upland regions.

The bogbean has two types of flowers, both of which are pink and white and star-shaped. In one, the pistil is long and the stamens short and hidden. In the other, the opposite is true, with a short pistil and long stamens. This arrangement makes self-pollination virtually impossible, but because stamens of one flower are at the same height as the pistil of another, cross-pollination by insects can take place.

Although it is of little economic importance now, at one time, our ancestors collected and ground up bogbean roots to make a flour which was widely used for bread-making. Leaves were used in a similar way to hops. Although both roots and leaves have a bitter taste, they were used in herbal remedies for rheumatism and jaundice.

Common in a wide variety of aquatic situations, undoubtedly the most noticeable feature of the greater reed-mace (*Typha latifolia*) are the thick reddish brown poker-like seed heads which appear in the early autumn and often remain in position until the following spring. The strong winds of February or March catch the pokers so that they release masses of light, silky white seeds. These are carried by the wind over long distances and, if they fall on suitable areas of soft mud, they will germinate.

Although the leaves die in the autumn, a creeping root stock ensures that growth begins again the next year. Long, narrow, grass-like leaves surround the stem, which eventually produces separate male and female flowers in July to August. Once the flower has been pollinated, the large seed will develop.

The water plantain's aerial leaves are different from the submerged ones. The latter develop first and are ribbon-shaped. The spoon-shaped aerial leaves arise from a rosette-like formation and are borne on long stalks. Flowers, white or reddish white in colour, appear from June to September.

Great reed-mace grows up from a creeping rhizome, full of stored starch. Because of its edible nature, it was almost certainly used by marsh-dwellers in former times. The relatively inconspicuous flowers are wind-pollinated. Although seeds are produced, the plant reproduces by means of shoots which grow out from the rhizome.

Established stands of bulrush along the inner edge of the emergent marsh vegetation are able to tolerate greater submersion than other species found in the same areas. The pithy stems have been used for floats and eel bobs. The flowering rush and the reed-mace often grow in close association.

The yellow flag is one of the most conspicuous of the marsh plants, with flowers and leaves typical of the iris family. Flowers can be seen from May to June. Insects, directed by dark brown honey guides on the petals, find nectar and incidentally bring about pollination.

The term 'bulrush' is often used to describe the reed-mace, but the true bulrush is *Schoenoplectus lacustris*. From the creeping rhizomes, submerged leaves sometimes arise, but generally most leaves grow out of the water, reaching a maximum height of 300 cm (118 in). From June to August, reddish-brown tinged flowering spikelets occur as a branched head.

The bulrush is sometimes used in thatching and weaving. When used in weaving the long stems produce tough mats and seating for rush-bottomed chairs.

The yellow flag (*Iris pseudacorus*), with its typical iris flowers, flourishes best where there is plenty of light. In heavy shade, flowers will not develop although the plant still grows each year. When the leaves die down in autumn, the thick rhizome remains dormant beneath the soil, ready to begin growth in the following spring. Extensive areas of rhizomes form an underground raft in marshy areas, allowing people to walk over an area in which they would otherwise sink.

The yellow flowers, which appear in May and June, have larger outer petals which are bent outwards and these are marked with brown-veined honey guides, which direct insects to the nectar, so that pollination can take place. Green pods containing the seeds can be seen in autumn. Ripe pods split open, scattering the buoyant reddish brown seeds which are carried by the water to new areas.

A member of the snapdragon family, the water-loving brooklime (*Veronica beccabunga*) is related to the germander and ivy-leaved speedwells, common plants of terrestrial habitats. In days past, the leaves, rich in vitamin C, were used in salads in spite of their bitter taste. In the past, herbalists, like Gerard, suggested many uses for it, including a cure for scurvy.

It is common in a variety of aquatic areas, including ponds, and wet places, and, if the creeping stems cannot root in the ground, they will float on the water. The flowers, held aloft on long stalks, are deep blue. Like other speedwells, it flowers from May through to September. On sunny days, the flowers open and insects bring about pollination. On dull days they remain closed and self-pollination occurs if the stigmas are touched by the stamens.

Where the marsh pennywort ((*Hydrocotyle vulgaris*)—also known as white rot—becomes established, its leaves carpet large areas of marshland. It grows in soft mud and in the water and spreads by creeping along the ground.

Long upright stalks are attached to the centre of the large round leaves, which measure up to 5 cm (2 in) across. Inconspicuous flowers arise from the stem on short stalks in uneven clusters. Very small and an indifferent greenish white in colour, they are often overlooked, even though they are on the plant for many months of the year.

Although each marsh helleborine (*Epipactis palustris*) produces only a solitary stem, where large numbers occur in damp situations amongst rushes, they are particularly attractive. Many plants may arise from one spreading underground rhizome. The leaves are narrow and those close to the ground are rounder than those on the upper parts, which taper into a point. On cold nights, dew collects in the cup-like structures, where each leaf joins the stem. This is valuable during drought conditions.

The outsides of the greenish-tinged sepals are covered with hairs. The wavy outline of the lower part of the flower lip provides a convenient landing platform for pollinating insects, such as burnet moths and bees.

The slender annual water pepper (*Polygonum hydropiper*) may reach a maximum height of 60 cm (24 in). The tapering, lance-like leaves have sheaths where they join the stem. The plant gets its name from the pungent peppery nature of the leaves, the juice of which may cause itching and even smarting when it gets on the skin.

It grows in shallow water and damp situations and the stem bears inconspicuous green flowers with almost imperceptible pink tinges. The small yellow dots on the petals are glands. The flowering period is from July to September.

In the least water pepper or small persicaria (*Polygonum minus*), the flowers are more distinctly pink and lack the yellow spots.

Frequenting many shady habitats, including marshy meadows as well as along banks, slow-flowing and still waters, the perennial water forget-me-not (*Myosotis palustris*) has a creeping rhizome which travels along the ground, sending out runners at intervals. The earliest attractive light blue flowers appear in May, the last in July. Each fruit consists of four shiny black nutlets.

A member of the Cruciferae, the flowers of the large bittercress (*Cardamine amara*) are arranged in the shape of a crucifix. It occurs in wet meadows and on streamsides. The flower petals tend to spread out and can be seen on the plants from April to June. It is related to the cuckoo flower.

A small unpretentious plant, blinks (*Montia verna*) has inconspicuous five-petalled greenish flowers which appear from April to October, although they are often obscured by the stems. Common in wet places, including wet meadows and streams in the south of Britain, it becomes increasingly rare towards the north. The hairless stems may creep along in the water or float on the surface and reach a length of 2–50 cm (0·8–20 in). Both annual and perennial forms are found.

Common marsh plants, most sedges belong to the large genus *Carex*. Some are seldom more than a few centimetres high whereas others may reach nearly 200 cm (79 in). Some sedges are on the lists of threatened species in several European countries. The Egyptians used the papyrus sedge (*Cyperus papyrus*) to make paper.

Perennials, sedges have triangular, usually solid stems with three-ranked leaves. Many leaves are rolled and, although it is not always immediately obvious, the margins of the leaves are saw-like.

Although many sedges grow in damp situations, others are found in dry habitats. Without competition from other plants, they may become the dominant vegetation in certain marshland habitats.

Beaked sedge or bottle sedge (*Carex rostrata*) is fairly widespread and sometimes grows in water. It reaches a height of between 30 and 60 cm (12 and 24 in) and the male and female flowers appear in June and July on separate plants.

The common sedge (*Carex nigra*) has underground rhizomes which enable it to creep over large areas. The separate male and female flowers appear from May to July. Common and widely distributed, the plants show a great deal of variation.

*Given suitable conditions, the marsh
helleborine produces creeping underground
shoots, enabling it to cover large areas.
From these shoots, the plant sends up
hundreds of flowering stems. The brown
and white flowers hang in loose clusters.
After fertilisation the large seeds develop
and float to new areas.*

*Where cyperus sedge occurs, it inhabits a variety of aquatic situations. The rough
triangular stem grows to a height of between 60 and 90 cm (24 and 36 in). The erect
male spikelets bear the flowers and the drooping ones bear the female flowers.*

Most sedges grow equally well in the marsh and other aquatic habitats. Sedges can be identified by their triangular stems. The terminal spike, called a panicle, is made up of a large number of stalked spikelets.

The soft rush commonly occurs in marshland. The underground rootstock pushes up a number of shoots, which are the stems. Leaves are not produced, but small brown scales appear at the bases of the stems and protect them.

The great marsh sedge or great pond sedge (*Carex riparia*) can be seen growing along the banks of ditches, rivers and canals, as well as in marshy areas and damp meadows. Beneath the soil, the tap roots send out a seemingly unending series of branches. The stem arising from the rootstock may reach a height of between 90 and 150 cm (36 and 60 in). The serrated-edged leaves are broader than those of many other species and extremely sharp. It flowers in May and June and the fruits develop after fertilisation.

The lesser pond sedge (*Carex acutiformis*) is similar to the previous species but does not grow as tall. The slender leaves are probably only half the width of those of the great marsh sedge.

The cyperus sedge (*Carex pseudocyperus*) is in flower along still watersides in marshes in May and June. Unlike many other sedges, its flowers are particularly noticeable. Male and female flowers, which are bright green in colour, appear on the same plant; the female ones droop distinctively. The fruits are a similar colour with a pronounced pointed beak and the seeds are prickly. The leaves measure up to 11 mm (0·4 in) at their broadest point and are an attractive pale green colour, with extremely sharp edges.

Two species of tufted sedge, (*Carex elata*) and (*Carex acuta*), are often mistaken for each other. *C.acuta* has a rhizome with underground runners. The smallest plants are 40 cm (16 in) high, but the tallest may grow to 100 cm (39 in).

The great panicled sedge or tussock sedge (*Carex paniculata*) is found over much of the British Isles but is more common in the south than the north. The large tussocks are particularly attractive, especially when in flower. The long broad leaves, with rough margins, often grow to greater lengths than the stems. With such a wide distribution, its growth rate is variable and in areas of poor soil or, perhaps, where competition is greater, it appears small and stunted, reaching no more than 30 cm (12 in). In more advantageous situations, it is a striking plant, attaining a height of between 120 and 150 cm (47 and 59 in). It flowers in June and July; male and female flowers, although separate, occur on the same spikelets.

The star sedge (*Carex echinata*) gets its name from its clusters of flowers, which are arranged in a star-shaped spike. Flowering from May to June in marshes, the smallest specimens may reach a height of no more than 10 cm (4 in); the taller ones grow up to 40 cm (16 in).

Of the few sedges which have any economic importance, the great fen sedge (*Cladium mariscus*), also known as the saw sedge, is perhaps the most important. In certain places, it has come to be known as the fenman's sedge and, of the numerous species of sedge, it alone used to be harvested. Where sufficient supplies were found, it was used for thatching the roofs of houses. If harvested annually, the yield is reduced, as an inferior crop results. The local people were fully aware that regular cutting weakened the plants and to prevent this, they were cut every fourth year only. The constant draining of the marshland habitat has greatly reduced its once widespread distribution, although it manages to retain a foothold in small undrained areas.

There are several species of cotton grass, but the common cotton grass (*Eriophorum angustifolium*) is the most widespread in the British Isles. Although described as a grass because of its leaf shape, it is a sedge. Shoots arise from a creeping root stock and the leaves, triangular in shape, tend to droop over. When stems grow out, they may reach 30 cm (12 in) in height, bearing a number of spikelets. On some plants there may be as few as two; on others up to seven. Most spikelets only have stalks, but where there are long smooth ones, the bright white heads hang from these. At a distance, these drooping heads appear to be flowers, but on closer examination they are seen to be hair-like bristles.

A sedge, although its name is misleading, the common spike rush (*Eleocharis palustris*) grows in a variety of habitats, from marshy land to the edges of ponds, lakes and ditches. The reddish brown root stock can creep over a wide area and, from it, tufts of numerous stiffly erect green stems grow. Some of the stems, which are pointed at the top, are flowerless, whereas others carry a single oval-shaped reddish brown spikelet from June to August.

Superficially resembling grasses, the rushes, which belong to the family Juncaceae, can be distinguished from their plant relatives by their long, narrow leaves, which are tough and rigid. In the past, they were sometimes collected and strewn on the floor of houses as a cheap and easily replaceable covering. They were, and still are, used to make matting, baskets and the seats of chairs. The Juncaceae is a small family of plants, containing about thirty British species in all. They are generally found in cold, damp areas, where they seem to flourish.

The two most common species are the soft rush (*Juncus effusus*) and the hard rush (*Juncus inflexus*) and, where they become established, they colonise large areas, forming dense tufts of sharp green leaves. Height varies between 60 and 90 cm (24 and 36 in). The leaves form sheaths at the base of the round erect stems. The leaves of the soft rush are distinctively green, whereas those of the hard rush have a perceptible bluish tinge. As their names imply, the stems of the soft rush are pliable whereas those of the hard rush are stiff and inflexible.

They are perennial plants and the underground rhizome is an effective propagation organ. The loosely structured, perfect (i.e. containing male and female organs) flowers are slightly to one side, arranged in clusters towards the apex of the stem. In this position, pollination by the wind is more likely. Both species flower from June.

The flowers of the conglomerate rush (*Juncus conglomeratus*) are more compact, forming a rounded ball-like inflorescence, when they appear in May. The alternative name of compact rush is an inevitable reference to the nature of the flower heads.

The sharp-flowered rush (*Juncus acutiflorus*) forms tall clumps with stiffly erect stems and reaches heights of up to 100 cm (39 in). The chestnut-brown flowers form tapering spikes and can be seen in July and August. Beneath the soil, the stout, spreading rhizomes increase the size of the clump considerably each year wherever conditions and habitat are favourable.

The marsh bedstraw (*Galium palustre*) has fewer flowers than the other common bedstraws. The leaves are generally arranged in fours or sixes, but unlike those of their relatives, they have rounded, rather than pointed ends. Flowering between June and August, it is common in many wet places.

Of the two stitchworts which occur, the marsh stitchwort (*Stellaria palus-*

The conglomerate rush sends up many
stems from a single underground rhizome.
This results in large clumps of plants. The
first flowers appear in May.

The reddish purple flowers of the marsh
woundwort appear from June to September
and are similar in shape and form to those
of nettles.

The marsh thistle bears its typical deep purple-red thistle flowers from June to September. These measure about 2 cm (0.7 in) across and after pollination will produce light seeds which will be carried by the wind to new areas.

The rare marsh sow thistle is found in the south-east of Britain. In spite of its rare status, it has increased in numbers where it has colonised dredged river banks.

tris) is found less frequently than the bog stitchwort (*Stellaria alsine*). The perennial bog stitchwort has square-shaped weak flowers. Each white flower has two petals and is smaller than those of the marsh stitchwort. Both species flower in early Summer.

Marsh cinquefoil (*Potentilla palustris*) is the only *Potentilla* in Britain which has purple flowers. Often found growing in damper areas of marshland, it is frequently associated with such species as rushes and bogbean. From the creeping rhizome, erect 15-45 cm (6-18 in) stems grow up. The purple-petalled flowers appear in the marsh from May to July.

The marsh violet (*Viola palustris*) differs from other violets in having more rounded leaves, but like the majority of other violets, the flowers have no scent. The creeping stem of this perennial throws up groups of hairless leaves, from the centre of which the flower stalk emerges. The flowers, which are pale lilac sometimes with darker streakings, have short spurs and can be seen from April to July.

The stems which arise from the underground rhizomes of the marsh woundwort (*Stachys palustris*) are mainly unbranched and may vary in height from 35-145 cm (14-57 in). The broadly lance-shaped leaves are heart-shaped at the base where they join the square stem. The edges are serrated and the surface of the leaf is covered with soft hairs. The pale purple flowers appear between June and September. Small swellings, tuber-like in shape, form on the rhizome and resemble the Chinese artichokes, which are obtained from another member of the same family.

The marsh thistle (*Cirsium palustre*), in flower from June to September, has smaller flowers than that of the creeping thistle. These develop in the leaf axils, as well as at the ends of the stems. Both male and female organs can be found in the same flower. The leaves are spiny with hairy upper surfaces.

The perennial marsh sowthistle (*Sonchus palustris*) only occurs in the south-east of Britain, where it is uncommon. Although rare, its position is not as precarious as it was towards the end of the last century, when it was feared that it would become extinct. It has colonised some areas of dredged river banks, which has expanded its habitat. Where conditions are particularly favourable, this tall species may reach a height of 240 cm (94 in). It has thicker stems than the corn sowthistle and smaller, less prickly teeth on the leaves. The pale yellow flowers are in bloom from July to August.

The marsh ragwort (*Senecio aquaticus*), with its composite flowers, belongs to the same family as the daisy. Growing to a height of between 30 and 75 cm (12 and 30 in), the branches grow out from the main stem. Towards the base of the plant, the leaves are either lobed or undivided. Those which grow higher up the plant are divided into leaflets clasping the stem. The flowers have outer ray florets and inner disc florets. The fruits have a parachute, or *pappus*, of white hairs which helps with their dispersal.

Now very rare, the marsh pea (*Lathyrus palustris*) is mainly confined to marshy areas of East Anglia. Lime in the soil is necessary if the plant is to flourish. The plant produces tendrils at the end of the stems, which it uses to attach itself to the reeds, thus to climb towards the light. When the bluish purple flowers fade, they are replaced by 2-5 cm (0·8-2 in) long seed pods.

Erect stems of the marsh horsetail (*Equisetum palustre*) grow up from a rhizome to a height of between 20 and 60 cm (8 and 24 in). The soft, grass-coloured stem bears a number of grooves, giving it a rough texture. Some stems bear sporangia, but these are indistinguishable from those which do not.

Marsh fleabane or common fleabane (*Pulicaria dysenterica*) does best in constantly grazed meadows of clay soils, although it occurs in other wet places and is widely distributed throughout the British Isles and Europe.

The stiff stems reach a height of between 30 and 60 cm (12 and 24 in) and are clasped firmly by the bases of the leaves. Numerous fine hairs on the undersurface of the leaves give them a cottony appearance. A strong unpleasant odour, described as a mixture of chrysanthemum and cat urine, seems to protect it from grazing animals.

The button-sized flowers have yellow centres surrounded by ray florets. At first, they are a rich golden colour, turning to brown when the seeds are produced. A parachute-like pappus aids seed dispersal.

A fore-runner of modern deodorisers, bunches of fleabane used to be hung in houses and ignited. Once lit, the smoke from the smouldering stems killed off insects, such as flies. It probably did not do a great deal for the people who inhaled its vapours!

Found mainly in southern counties, water betony (*Scrophularia aquatica*), or water figwort, is common in wet places. It is related to figwort, although it is taller and more substantial, reaching a height of between 50 and 100 cm (20 and 40 in). The plant has an unpleasant smell. The small dots which can be seen on the leaf stems are glands. The flowers appear from June to September. The leaves were once crushed and mixed with fat to form an ointment, which was applied to swellings to reduce their size.

The common valerian (*Valeriana officinalis*) occurs widely in damp areas, but the marsh valerian (*Valeriana dioica*) is less common. Both are perennials. The common valerian grows to heights of between 30 and 150 cm (12 and 60 in). The marsh valerian seldom manages more than 30 cm (12 in). Both upright and creeping stems are produced. Male and female flowers are found on different plants.

In spite of its rather unpleasant smell, common valerian was a much sought-after medicinal herb. It had many uses, ranging from the prevention of hysteria to the relief of headaches. It was specially grown in certain counties for use by herbalists. Valerian tea, although drunk in the British Isles, was more popular in Germany.

Two species of bur-marigolds may be found in marshland areas. Both are summer-flowering annuals which grow in muddy margins around areas of water. The nodding bur-marigold (*Bidens cernua*) gets its name from the nodding habits of the flower heads. In the rayed nodding bur-marigold (*Bidens cernua* var. *radiata*), the flower heads are surrounded by rays, similar to those of the sunflower. In general, however, the flowers are small and greenish yellow and not particularly conspicuous. Both male and female organs appear on the same flower. The seeds have a number of sharp barbs by which they become attached to animals' fur and birds' feathers. When irritation occurs, the creature scratches, removing the seeds, which are thus dispersed to new areas. It is locally common, preferring situations where there is only winter standing water.

A member of the Compositae, the marsh ragwort has golden-yellow flowers, composed of twelve to fifteen florets. It is a typical member of this group, which also includes the familiar dandelion. The seeds, being light, are carried long distances in wind currents.

The growth of marsh fleabane is stimulated in places where grazing occurs. Grazing animals tend to avoid the fleabane because of its unpleasant smell but eat other plants. Thus it can grow unhindered.

Much less common than the closely-related common valerian, the marsh valerian is a perennial species. The five-petalled flowers appear from May to June and, once pollinated, wither. The resulting fruits have a single seed.

Intensive drainage of wetlands has led to a serious decline in the numbers of the snake's head fritillary. After dispersal, the seeds become established most successfully in habitats which are grazed regularly.

The flowers of the water mint can be found from July to August. At other times of the year the plant is inconspicuous, except for the pleasant smell which is released when it is trampled on. This seems to linger in the marshland, particularly on still, damp days.

The bright yellow flowers of the marsh marigold are composed of five sepals, not petals, as in most other flowers. Flowering early in the marsh, they add a brightness to the scene before many other species have appeared.

The snake's head fritillary (*Fritillaria meleagris*) has been affected by wetland drainage and has become rare in some places. A frequent species in the wet meadows around marshland in the east and south of the British Isles, it still makes a tenacious stand in some of its old-established haunts, although it has vanished from many others.

The particularly attractive flowers are borne on stems from 21–45 cm (8–18 in) high, towards the end of April. The nodding purple or white bells, some 32–50 mm (1·2–2 in) long, usually occur in twos. Summer grazing is beneficial to the plant once the seeds have been dispersed because the seedlings make better headway where the sward is short.

Found in wet places throughout the country, common skullcap (*Scutellaria galericulata*) has hairy stems which may reach a height of 45 cm (18 in). Although this perennial species may creep along the ground, it generally grows upright. The opposite lance-shaped leaves are attached to the stem by very short stalks. The blue to violet flowers, which appear in the marsh from June to September, grow out from the leaf axil on one side of the stem.

No plant is more characteristically aromatic in marshes than the water mint (*Mentha aquatica*). Trampling through marshy areas, the distinctive minty aroma pervades the air as the leaves and stems of the plant are crushed. In bloom from July to August, the lilac flowers attract hordes of butterflies and bees. The main flowers are arranged in a spherical head on the end of the stems. Other less well developed flowers grow out from the leaf axils.

Water mint was crossed with the green spearmint to produce the plant from which peppermint is extracted. It is a useful medicinal herb which is supposed to cure migraine and also settles indigestion. Gipsies used to collect the leaves and make a drink from them.

The red-veined dock or wood dock (*Rumex sanguineus*) and the closely related sharp dock (*Rumex conglomeratus*) both grow in damp situations. The wood dock has a more erect stem than that of the sharp dock and it bears fewer leaves between the flower whorls. The sharp dock, known alternatively as the clustered dock, reaches a height of between 30–60 cm (12 and 24 in). It is a perennial species, with flower stalks arranged up the stem, interspersed with leafy bracts.

If no grazing animals nibble at it, the hemp agrimony (*Eupatorium cannabinum*) survives in a variety of damp situations, including marshes. It flowers from July to August and the stem which bears the inflorescences grows up to 120 cm (47 in) tall. The large numbers of flowers vary from reddish mauve to white. Butterflies seek out this species, attracted not only by the nectar, but possibly also by the colour. Because the underground rootstock sends up numerous new shoots each year, in suitable conditions the plant grows in large patches.

At first sight, the marsh marigold (*Caltha palustris*) may be taken for a buttercup, with its yellow buttercup-like flowers, but the flowers are, in fact, larger than those of its relative. The alternative name, kingcup, is appropriate because the golden flowers brighten the dull marshland vegetation.

Where the reed-cutter has been at work, the kingcup flowers before the reeds have a chance to grow again. Generally flowering from March to May, some plants still have flowers in August.

Glossy heart-shaped leaves grow from the thick creeping root stock. Once the flowers have faded, the leaves increase in size, producing large amounts of food, some of which is used for growth, the rest being stored in the root stock. The plant has been known for a long time as its numerous common names demonstrate. In fact it has been growing here since before the last Ice Age.

Early in the year, insects are attracted to the bright nectar-producing flowers and butterflies waking from hibernation take their share. It is the bright yellow sepals, not petals, which give the flower its distinctive colour. After pollination, the seeds develop in pod-like follicles and, when ripe, they are released and dispersed by water.

The marsh marigold produces the poison protoanemonine, a substance found in some other members of the buttercup family. Although the amounts are small, it is unpleasant and cattle avoid the plant. In days gone by, the flower heads were collected, pickled in vinegar and used instead of Mediterranean capers. Juice from the plant was once used to colour butter.

Growing to a height of nearly 150 cm (59 in), the perennial water parsnip (*Sium latifolium*) grows amongst other vegetation, single plants being usual. From the rhizome, shoots appear which eventually bear umbels, producing flowers in July and August.

A member of the parsley family, the umbelliferous wild angelica (*Angelica sylvestris*) needs damp situations and is found in marshy areas. The purple stem is grooved and hollow. The white flowers, sometimes pinkish tinged, are to be found from June to September. A perennial, the plants may reach a height of between 150 and 250 cm (59 and 98 in).

Several species of the poisonous dropworts belonging to the umbelliferous parsley family may be found in and around the marsh. Water dropwort (*Oenanthe fistulosa*) grows in ditches and wet places, where it flowers from July to September. The generally white blossoms sometimes have a pinkish tinge. Smooth, hollow stems arise from underground tubers, which are swollen with stored food. Toward's the base of the plant, the leaves are fern-like, whereas those further up are much narrower and are held on long stalks.

Sometimes the fine-leaved water dropwort (*Oenanthe aquatica*) grows in water, in which case the submerged leaves have much narrower segments, an adaptation to ensure that flowing water will not damage them.

Parsley water dropwort (*Oenanthe lachenalii*) has almost solid ribbed stems which differentiate it from the water dropwort. Flowering from July to September, it grows in similar situations.

Compared with the previous species, the hemlock water dropwort (*Oenanthe crocata*) has a much stouter stem, which arises from the underground tubers. Taller specimens reach a height of 200 cm (79 in). The leaves are larger than those of the other three species and the upper ones are much more divided. The flowers, which can be seen on the plant from June to September, occur in smaller clusters than in the other species.

The milk parsley or hog's fennel (*Peucedanum palustre*) is an important plant in the Broads of East Anglia, where it provides food for the caterpillars of the swallowtail butterfly (see p. 87). An umbellifer, the hollow stem supports a number of white flowers from July to September. The leaves are broad-lobed and finely-toothed.

In the Norfolk Broads, the milk parsley is particularly important, because it is one of the sources of food for the caterpillars of the swallowtail butterfly. An umbellifer, it is also known as hog's fennel.

In the butterbur, the flowers appear before the leaves. It belongs to the same family as the daisies and each flower head is composed of a number of florets. Each spike consists of either male or female flowers. The first flowers appear in March and the last ones have usually vanished by the end of May.

There is a distinctive and unmistakable smell carried on the breeze where there are stands of meadowsweet. It is not only the scent which attracts the attention of man in the marsh, but the delightful nature of the creamy flowers.

The southern marsh orchid is a close relative of the group collectively labelled 'early marsh orchids'. It is undoubtedly a hybrid, probably between the early marsh orchid (Dactylorhiza incarnata) and the common and heath spotted orchids (D. fuchsii and D. maculata).

Native to North America, the orange balsam (*Impatiens capensis*) was brought to Britain in the last century, and is now found in many marshes, as well as along the banks of rivers. Seeds produced in the autumn germinate in the following spring and, by June, the plant has reached a height of between 90 and 130 cm (35 and 51 in).

The showy orange species, like all the balsams, has a distinctive flower, characterised by a small upper hood with a spur below and a broad lower lip. They first appear in July and stay on the plant until killed by the first frosts. A plentiful supply of white pollen adheres to the bodies of the many insects, mainly bees and wasps, which visit the flowers, ensuring that pollination occurs.

The flowers of the butterbur (*Petasites hybridus*) appear before the leaves. The plant is a member of the daisy family and so the flower head consists of many individual flowers, each either male or female, although in some parts of the British Isles all male flowers may occur on an individual plant. Where this happens no seeds are produced. In a few northern counties, female flowers seem to predominate, with some male ones occurring so that pollination can take place.

The large long-stalked leaves are unmistakable. They are pink-veined, with a distinctly wrinkled surface, and may grow to over 100 cm (39 in) long. Both surfaces of the young leaves are covered with hairs, but these disappear from the undersurface as they grow. At one time, folk used to collect the leaves for wrapping up their butter, hence its common name. The powdered root, when added to wine, was supposed to help bring down the temperature of people suffering from fevers.

Its former name 'queen of the meadow' aptly describes the meadowsweet (*Filipendula ulmaria*). When in full bloom in summer, it tends to overshadow everything else in the marsh, not only with its delightful creamy flowers, but also with its scent.

The name 'meadowsweet', although admirably suited to this plant, is actually a corruption of 'meadsweet', because it was once used to flavour mead. Culpepper suggested that a leaf from the plant added that something extra to a glass of claret. It was also used by the early herbalists for treating malaria. In the past, the meadowsweet was often strewn on floors, along with other plants; a slightly carbolic smell resulted when the leaves were crushed. The Shetlanders called it 'courtship and matrimony' because the smell changed once the leaves were trodden on.

A member of the rose family, meadowsweet is often confused with the parsleys, although the flower heads are not arranged in the typical umbellifer fashion of these plants. It is often mown and used with hay, as cattle relish its astringent qualities. Mowing only delays the arrival of the flowers, which make their appearance in the autumn.

Several species of orchids are particularly associated with marshy areas. These are the early marsh orchid or meadow orchid (*Dactylorhiza incarnata*) and the common marsh orchid or fen orchid (*Dactylorhiza majalis praetermissa*). The former found in many damp places comes into flower before the common marsh orchid. Although the flowers are considered generally to be pink, there is a wide colour variation including dark red, white and even yellow. Large numbers of flowers are clustered onto the cylindrical spikes. The petals resemble wings and the yellowish green rigid leaves, although narrow, are sword-shaped.

Although the common marsh orchid has suffered because of the drainage of wetlands, it is still relatively common in suitable habitats, especially in southern Britain. As with its relative, flower colour is very variable, from the typical pinkish purple, to white. The flower spike has a more cone-shaped form than the early marsh orchid. Identification from the leaves is difficult, because, although generally without spots, some hybridisation has occurred between the species and the spotted orchid.

A further species, generally confined to northern areas is the northern fen orchid (*Dactylorhiza majalis purpurella*). The leaves are more stunted and generally unmarked, although spotted varieties have been recorded. A solid stem holds the short spike of reddish purple flowers upright.

The widespread common spotted orchid (*Dactylorhiza fuchsii*) is found in many damp situations, reaching heights of between 15 and 60 cm (6 and 24 in). Before the flowers appear, they are protected by a series of grass-like bracts. They can be seen from early spring to early summer as oblong spikes, the colours of which vary from pale purple to lilac.

Leaf shape varies, the lowest ones are blunt in outline, above these oval ones occur and the uppermost ones are narrow and taper to a point. They are green in colour with purple spots.

A member of the pink family, the ragged robin (*Lychnis flos-cuculi*) grows in many damp situations, flourishing where taller plants do not shade out the light, and can reach a height of 60 cm (24 in).

The ragged magenta-coloured flowers appear on the plant from May to July. More than 30 mm (1·2 in) across, they are held on rather slender stems. The middle one in each terminal cluster opens first. They produce a good supply of nectar and a wide variety of insects, including bumblebees, visit them. In the Norfolk Broads, the swallowtail also takes its fill of nectar. By carrying pollen from one plant to another, insects bring about cross-pollination. This is further ensured because, in any one flower, the anthers produce all their pollen before the stigmas are exposed. The seeds develop in a dry capsule.

The guelder rose (*Viburnum opulus*) becomes well established in marshes, especially where there is some lime in the soil. The white flowers appear in June and are particularly attractive. The brilliant white outer flowers are sterile. The inner, less conspicuous, fertile flowers have a pinkish tinge when they are in bud but become pale yellowish cream once they unfold. It is the inner flowers which produce the attractive red, shiny berries in the autumn. The unusual flower scent was described by an earlier herbalist as like 'peppered trout'. Many night-flying moths come to the flowers for nectar, assisting with pollination.

As the leaves begin to change colour towards the end of summer, they are particularly attractive, producing many shades of red, from crimson through to scarlet, on the same bush. Where the autumn light catches the tree, it appears to be on fire.

The common rosebay willow herb (*Epilobium angustifolium*) may be

Although the rosebay willow herb is widely distributed in the marsh, the great hairy willow herb, together with the marsh willow herb, is the more typical species. The great hairy willow herb is known as 'codlins and cream' in many areas, although the origin of this name is uncertain.

The celery-leaved crowfoot (or buttercup) is a member of the Ranunculaceae. The typical yellow buttercup flowers, each with five narrow petals, occur in a terminal spike and appear on the plant between May and September.

Known either as sweet gale or bog myrtle,
this plant is a shrub which may reach a
height of 120 cm (48 in). The flowers,
known as catkins, appear on the plant in
April, before the leaves have been released
from their buds. Individual plants usually
have either male or female flowers.

Although the globe flower belongs to the
buttercup family, its flowers are not
typical of the buttercup. Appearing from
May to June, they resemble miniature
yellow globes and have numerous nectaries,
which attract a host of insects.

found in marshes, but the marsh willow herb (*Epilobium palustre*) and the great hairy willow herb (*Epilobium hirsutum*) are more typical of this habitat. The former is much less conspicuous. A perennial, the marsh willow herb has somewhat hairy stems and reaches a height of between 15 and 60 cm (6 and 24 in). The leaves are narrow and opposite. It flowers from June to August and is locally common in marshland areas. The great hairy willow herb is also known as 'codlins and cream', although how it came by this name is a mystery. It might be from the smell of the crushed leaves, which is reminiscent of the codlin apple, or because the flower looks like coddled apples—an old-fashioned dish of apples boiled in milk.

The celery-leaved crowfoot (*Ranunculus sceleratus*) and the creeping buttercup (*Ranunculus repens*) occur in marshlands. The creeping buttercup is an annual species and, although smaller, is similar to the more common bulbous buttercup (*Ranunculus bulbosa*). It can be distinguished by its hairier paler leaves. The flowers are also smaller and paler in colour.

The hollow stems of the celery-leaved crowfoot contain a bitter-tasting liquid which is so strong that once on the skin it may cause blisters. In the past, tramps and beggars actually rubbed it onto their skin to induce blisters, so that, when begging, people would take pity on them because of the blisters. Some botanists have suggested that the Latin name *sceleratus*, which means 'wicked', might refer to this practice.

The plant does well where there is thick mud, rich in nutrients and, in such situations, it can reach a height of 45 cm (18 in). In other areas, it may be no more than 15 cm (6 in) tall. The flowers, which are the smallest of any buttercup, are borne from May to September.

A member of the buttercup family, the greater spearwort (*Ranunculus lingua*) often grows singly in amongst other emergent vegetation, as well as in ditches. The leaves found on non-flowering shoots are heart-shaped, with long stalks. On flowering shoots, the leaves are much narrower and have shorter stalks.

Typical buttercup-coloured golden-yellow flowers appear from June to August. They measure up to 5 cm (2 in) across, which is larger than many of the other common buttercups. It is a typical if uncommon marshland plant, reaching a height of 60 cm (24 in).

The globe flower (*Trollius europaeus*) is a member of the buttercup family, although its flowers are not typical. About 2·5 cm (1 in) across, the flowers appear from May to August and have no green sepals. Inside the flower, as many as fifteen nectaries attract pollinating insects. After pollination, the small black seeds which develop are contained in follicles. Not a particularly common member of the buttercup family, the globe flower will be found in damp meadows besides marshes.

Bog myrtle or sweet gale (*Myrica gale*) is a small shrub varying between 60 and 120 cm (24 and 48 in) in height. The flowers (catkins) first appear in April, before the leaves, and each plant generally bears either all male or all female flowers. After fertilisation, small two-winged seeds develop. The leaves have small yellow spots on their surface. These are glands which produce an aromatic scent, as one of its common names suggests. On marshes where it is common, its strong smell on a warm evening is an unforgettable scent.

The dog rose (*Rosa canina*) occurs in the drier parts of the marsh and along walls and river banks. The thorns on the stem are an efficient defence. There are several species of dog rose, all flowering from June to July, and it is difficult to differentiate between them. The familiar pink or white flowers, from which all modern roses have been bred, attract many insects with their sweet scent. Later in the year, the well known rose hips develop, containing a rich supply of vitamin C, which is used in the production of rose hip syrup. Most, however, will be taken for food by birds and mammals.

There are more than 400 varieties of the bramble (*Rubus fruticosus*), which quickly establishes itself in drier areas of the marsh. The flowers take a variety of form and, after they have flowered between June and August, a crop of blackberries develop, which are much sought after by both man and beast in the autumn.

The larger bindweed (*Calystegia sepium*) may be encountered in some parts of the marsh as frequently as in other habitats. Using a variety of plants for support, the bindweed winds its stem around its 'host' in an anti-clockwise direction. The large, showy white bell-shaped flowers can be seen for several months between June and October.

Ever eager to find a niche where there is a support, the honeysuckle (*Lonicera periclymenum*) has the alternative name of woodbine, because of its habit of twining itself around other plants. The sweet-scented flowers, in bloom from June to September, are visited by night-flying moths, which, while taking their share of nectar, also effect pollination. Opening at twilight, the flowers are either white, cream or delicately pink, until they are pollinated, when they become orange-brown.

Known also as bittersweet, the woody nightshade (*Solanum dulcamara*) has flowers which are similar to those of the potato, to which it is closely related. A straggling species, it is in flower from June to September. A poisonous drug is obtained from the stem.

Red campion (*Melandrium rubrum*) is a common and very showy plant which has established itself in certain marshland areas. Male and female flowers are on separate plants and have no scent. The white and red species often cross-pollinate to produce a pink-flowered form.

Growing in the marsh and by the sides of rivers, the purple loosestrife (*Lythrum salicaria*) reaches a height of between 100 and 130 cm (39 and 51 in). Different types of flowers are produced, with varying lengths of stamens and styles. As insects visit the flowers, they pick up pollen from short, medium or long stamens and transfer it to stamens of the same length on another flower.

A plant of moist places, the yellow loosestrife (*Lysimachia vulgaris*) is never more than about 130 cm (51 in) high and flourishes best in southern areas. The yellow flowers have red stamens. It is not related to the purple loosestrife.

The moist marshland habitat also proves suitable for several species of moss. Unless surrounded by water, moss becomes dessicated and water is also necessary for reproduction to take place.

Willow moss (*Fontinalis antipyretica*) is an aquatic species living in lakes and rivers. Its long, irregularly branched stems may reach 100 cm (39 in) in length. The ripe spores are produced in summer.

63

The distinctive flowers of the purple loosestrife appear from June to August. Each flower is composed of six magenta petals.

Another aquatic species is the rare *Drepanocladus aduncus*, which is found in pools and marshes. The leaves vary in colour from golden through to green. The spores ripen in the summer months.

By far the most common species are the *Sphagnum* mosses, which are found in almost any damp place: the banks of rivers, streams, ponds, lakes and ditches and even in water. In drought conditions, *Sphagnum* remains moist, because many of its cells are capable of storing moisture.

Like the mosses, the liverworts need water for survival and reproduction. Several species occur in the marsh, few of which have common names. In some, the leaf-like thallus and stems can be seen: in others these are not apparent.

The rare floating crystalwort (*Riccia fluitans*) occurs in ponds and ditches as two forms, one which floats on the water and one which grows on mud, sending out root-like rhizoids. These are not seen in flowering specimens.

Marchantia polymorpha is found along stream banks and in marshes, where it often forms large patches. The dark green, creeping thallus is between 2 and 10 cm (1 and 4 in) long and has a particularly noticeable mid-rib. This species reproduces either by kidney-shaped buds, called *gemmae*, or by spores.

Found on wet rocks along the sides of streams, the great scented liverwort (*Conocephalum conicum*) has a pleasant smell when crushed.

Pellia epiphylla is a common liverwort in marshes and typical of this group of plants. The male and female organs occur on the same thallus which is anchored to the ground by rhizoids. The sperm-making male sex organs develop on the upper surface of the thallus, whereas the female egg-producing ones can be seen at its tip. Water is necessary for fertilisation to take place as it allows the sperms to swim towards the eggs. The spores develop inside a capsule called a *sporophyte* and, once ripe, they are liberated and carried by the wind to new areas where they develop into new plants.

The marsh fern (*Thelypteris palustris*) is a perennial species, which has creeping underground rhizomes and reaches a height of between 25 and 75 cm (10 and 30 in). The plant can be found in marshy areas, especially where there is shelter from trees. It is particularly noticeable between July and August.

Trees

SEVERAL SPECIES OF TREES are associated with wetland habitats and thus with marshland, particularly willows and alder. Alder carr, in fact, is the climax marsh vegetation, although its development takes a long time. However, with the draining of vast stretches of marshland, the trees typically associated with such areas will either decrease in numbers or die out. In the past, marshland trees were a valuable resource and, indeed, they still provide raw materials for various craft industries today.

The downy birch or hairy birch (*Betula pubescens*) is less common than silver birch. In some places it has the alternative name of white birch. It needs damp ground and marshes provide it with a suitable niche. Although the leaves are downy or hairy, this characteristic can be misleading because, where it grows with silver birch (*Betula pendula*), hybrids may appear. Although it does grow in close association with other species of birch, it is generally the downy birch species which is found in marshy places.

The bark covering the twigs varies in colour from brown to a delicate purplish tinge. The small scales on the buds, which are usually liberally covered with white hairs, begin to peel back in April. The leaves are supported on long stalks and have a stickier surface than those of silver birch. In birches generally, the leaves vary in shape from oval to triangular, but all have a pointed tip and a serrated edge. In the majority of downy birch trees, the leaves are either wedge-shaped or round and, usually, the pointed apex is less pronounced. The undersurface of most of the leaves has a coat of hairs.

The male catkins appear on the tree in autumn, but the female ones do not appear until late March or April of the following year. In the autumn, these male flowers are relatively small and not particularly distinctive because of their drab brownish grey colour. They begin to enlarge in the spring, becoming pendulous when fully developed. Their rich supply of golden pollen makes them particularly conspicuous. When the female flowers have been pollinated, numerous small winged seeds develop. These are liberated in the autumn. The seeds are very light in weight and the wind may carry them far afield. If they land in suitably damp conditions, the seeds will germinate in the following spring.

The downy birch tree is not known for longevity or size and specimens in excess of 33 m (105 ft) are the exception rather than the rule. It is susceptible to the ravages of the parasitic bracket fungus, *Piptoporus* (=*Polyporus*) *betulinus*, which shorten its life considerably. Once this fungus is established, the mycelia invade the tree, taking nourishment from its tissues, Death will eventually result and trees which are hosts to the bracket fungus seldom live for more than 60 years.

As with so many of our native trees, the use of the common ash (*Fraxinus excelsior*) as a timber tree has decreased greatly since the Industrial Revolution, as iron and steel have taken its place. The ash is found in many areas of the British Isles and over much of Europe and does well in marshy habitats, because it needs a continuous supply of moisture.

The conical, hard jet-black buds are unmistakable and the ash can be recognised easily in winter when it is leafless. Before the buds open, they have an almost velvety appearance. The first leaves normally appear towards the end of April and the tree is finally regaled in green by May.

The compound leaves have an overall length of 15 cm (6 in) and consist of 9–15 leaflets, each with a serrated edge. As autumn approaches, the leaves undergo a variety of indescribable colour changes, usually turning yellow in September and falling from the tree by the end of October.

As the tree ages, changes in the bark colour may cause some confusion. The bark is grey and smooth on the young tree but, as the tree matures, it gradually changes to brown and develops numerous uneven interwoven ridges.

The catkin-like flowers appear on the tree before the leaves open and it is their colour which gives the tree its characteristic purplish tinge. Which flowers a tree will bear each year is virtually impossible to predict. Some trees have all male flowers, others all female ones. On some specimens, there are male flowers on some branches one year and female ones in the following year. There are trees with perfect flowers, i.e. bearing both male and female parts. The wind is an effective pollinator, carrying pollen from the male stamens to the female pistils. After fertilisation, a single seed begins to develop from each flower, eventually forming the characteristic ash key. These keys are a prominent feature of the tree in September, when clusters of them can be seen on the branches. At first they are green, but by October they have changed to brown and are ready to fall from the tree. Some remain until the following year. The single twisted wing enables the seed to be carried far away by the wind. Some birds and small mammals will eat the seeds and thus effect their dispersal.

Like the willows, the common alder or black alder (*Alnus glutinosa*) is a tree typically associated with wetland habitats. The alder flowers or catkins first open on the tree in March. Typically, the female catkins are small; seldom greater than 8 mm (0·3 in) long. They stand upright on the tree and the tiny reddish brown scales cover two flowers. When viewed on the tree in winter, they are extremely small, inconspicuous cylindrical-shaped structures. The male catkins are much more conspicuous. They are pendulous and about 5–10 cm (2–4 in) long. After pollination, the fruits begin to develop, swelling throughout the summer, until they eventually form the familiar cones which ripen by the autumn. As the cones develop, their colour changes from green to black. Although smaller, they bear a superficial resemblance to the cones found on conifers but, as the alder is not directly related to these evergreen species, alder cones are referred to as 'false cones'. Seeds which are not scattered from the cones are taken by birds and empty cones may be seen for much of the winter and well into the following spring. Leafless during adverse conditions, alders are usually easy to identify because of the persistence of the cones.

Once released, the seeds are admirably adapted for dispersal by aquatic means in the following spring. In the water they can survive for about a month; small airtight cavities keep them afloat. Aquatic birds, including ducks, eat the alder seeds and thus assist their dispersal; strong winds also spread them. The seeds germinate most easily in soft mud.

The pointed, purple-coloured buds are a distinctive feature of the tree.

The leaves unfold in about May and ultimately measure between 5 and 7 cm (2 and 2·75 in) both wide and long. When they first begin to unfold, they have a distinctly tacky feel, hence the Latin name of *glutinosa*. The leaves of many deciduous trees change colour before they fall, but there is no such colour change in the alder and the falling leaves are green.

The rough black bark hides a soft timber, which when first exposed to the light is white, but when left to season develops a reddish tinge. Because it is soft, the timber has little commercial value. It has been useful in the past for piles and bridge supports because it does not rot under water. Other earlier uses include barrel-making and clog-making and, at one time, it was burned to form charcoal, which was used extensively in gunpowder. Today it is used for small toys, the handles of tools and half-round broom heads.

Fully-grown alders never reach a great height, the tallest being around 21 m (67 ft). The coppicing of many alders to provide poles stunts their growth.

Early in its life, the alder grows quite quickly. Because its roots are able to fix nitrogen from the atmosphere, it has no problems in surviving in marshy conditions, where soil nitrogen is at a premium. It is because the alder can fix nitrogen and release any excess into the soil that areas where it grows are very fertile. In earlier times, it grew extensively in the East Anglian fens and this part of the British Isles owes much of its subsequent fertility to this tree.

The tap root may be up to 150 cm (59 in) long, which helps the tree to obtain enough moisture when the water level falls. Today, the alder's chief value lies in the stabilising effect which it has on the banks of water courses, where it often prevents what might otherwise be excessive erosion.

Because the alder buckthorn (*Frangula alnus*) is a relatively small tree, it is frequently overlooked in the damp areas where it grows. Specimens generally vary in height from 1·5–3 m (5–10 ft). Its name is misleading, since it is not a member of the alder family and is thornless. In some places, it is known as the berry-bearing alder, because the leaves, although smaller, can be mistaken for those of the alder.

It is probable that the plant's inappropriate name of buckthorn is due to a past misunderstanding. The German word for bush was *Buxdorn*, which, if properly translated, would have given 'box-thorn', but with its lack of thorns this would also have been misleading.

The whitish green flowers have both male and female parts and open in late May or early June. Black berries will develop from the fertilised flowers and will be evident in September. At one time, unripe berries were collected and, from them, a good quality dye was extracted and used for printing designs onto calico.

Some of the straighter stems were used for the centre stays in umbrellas and for fashioning into walking sticks. It was burnt for a charcoal which was

Seeds of alders germinate easily and the tree is seldom deliberately planted. Appearing in March, the drooping male catkins are between 5 and 10 cm (2 and 4 in) long, whereas the female ones are much smaller, seldom more than 0·8 mm (0·3 in) in length. The latter are upright and both flowers are covered in red scales.

considered superior to that obtained from the alder. Where it was cut and processed in this way it was known as black dogwood.

The female of the brimstone butterfly lays her eggs on the leaves of alder buckthorn (see p. 90).

Willows (*Salix* spp.) flourish where the ground is wet, establishing themselves in conditions which few other species can tolerate. Undoubtedly, one of the greatest difficulties with this group of trees is accuracy in identification, because hybridisation is common and the offspring exhibit characteristics of each parent species. This fact, coupled with the varieties produced for commercial reasons, leaves a bewildering number of species for the amateur to identify.

Few species of willows grow to tree height, the majority only reaching shrub size. Although willow timber provides little worthwhile wood, other parts of the tree are valuable in various crafts (see p. 16).

Of the willows frequently encountered in marshland areas, only the crack willow, white willow, and sallow (also known as goat willow) are particularly common, although other species, such as the almond-leaved willow, bay willow and common or grey sallow are found. Three of these species—the crack willow, white willow and sallow—can be considered as timber trees.

Although willows grow quickly, the light timber which results is, nevertheless, reasonably tough. Osiers are also members of the willow family and provide various craftsmen with material for making baskets, crab pots, lobster pots and hampers. They are grown commercially in osier beds, where suitable pliant shoots develop and are cut for craftwork. Baskets have always been in fashion and the demand for osiers continues to flourish, in spite of alternative man-made fibres.

Willow bark has been valued for a very long time and salicin has been extracted from it for centuries for its astringent and tonic qualities. Salicin is also an ingredient of aspirin.

Willows are seldom allowed to attain their natural height, the tops being pollarded—cut out at a height of about 200 cm (80 in) above the ground—to encourage the growth of long, thin, pliant shoots; these can then be cut and used for coarse basket-making. The lance-shaped leaves with finely serrated margins may be up to 10 cm (4 in) in length. Most willow trees are single-sexed and male and female flowers are borne on separate trees. On rare occasions, some branches on the same tree may bear male flowers and others female ones.

Willows take well from cuttings and the tree which grows will be of the same sex as that from which the shoot was taken. Where willow is used for posts, it often 'strikes', producing a line of willow trees.

The catkins of most willows open in March, making the trees clearly visible before any leaves appear on the trees. A colourful display of catkins indicates that spring is on the way. It is from the catkins that some willows get their common country name, 'pussy willow'. Their soft, downy nature and white hairs are reminiscent of the fur of the domestic cat. Both male and female catkins are oval in shape.

Both insects and wind are responsible for transferring the pollen from the male to the female flowers. When ripe, the anthers of the male flowers have a beautiful golden sheen, which contrasts sharply with the greenish grey almost silvery appearance of the female flowers. Nectaries producing sweet-tasting liquid attract insects, with early visitors finding a plentiful supply, particularly at this time of the year when there are few other flowers to provide nourishment.

After pollination, the seeds develop, ripening by the middle of summer. Each seed has a tuft of hair which helps it to become airborne. It then depends on the wind for its dispersal. If the seed is to grow, it must germinate quickly, since its life span is variously described as being from as little as 18 hours to as long as 3 weeks.

Willow leaves come in a great variety of shapes. In some species, they are lance-shaped, in others oval and yet others have a rounded outline. If the group does not have a commonly distinctive leaf shape, at least the buds have a consistent feature. They are oval in shape with only one external scale leaf, which is smooth to the touch.

The white willow (*Salix alba*) owes its name to the colour of its leaves. Light reflecting off the numerous hairs which cover the leaf give it a greyish white appearance. If this species is allowed to grow to its natural dimensions, it can be one of our most beautiful trees. The tree is often left to its own devices. At one time the bark was considered almost as valuable as that of oak for tanning purposes.

The pollarded willows common in southern and midland Britain are generally white willows. Although the timber from the tree is of little value, farmers lop the tops every 2 years or so. The pliant twigs are used for a variety of purposes, including hurdle-making, and the rougher lengths are used to fill in holes in hedges and fences.

In the past, the soft, easily-worked wood from the white willow found a ready friend in both the turner and the carver. Dairy and household utensils, such as bowls and plates, as well as the well-known Sussex trug baskets, were all shaped from this timber. Yokes, so ably worn by milk-maids in earlier days, were often made from willow; artificial limbs were also made from the wood. Modern materials have replaced the willow in many of these items but the Sussex trugs are still as popular as ever.

None of these products will ever be as famous as the cricket-bat, lovingly shaped from the cricket-bat willow, a variety of white willow, known botanically as *Salix alba* var. *coerulea*. These trees are not found in marshland areas, but are grown in selected meadows and farmed for their valuable timber.

The crack willow (*Salix fragilis*) owes its unusual name to a characteristic of its twigs. When pulled back sharply they will break off the tree with an audible 'crack'. Although this property distinguishes the crack willow from other species, it does not appear to have any value except in propagation. High winds may break off twigs, tossing them away from the tree to take root far from the parent plant.

Leaves of the crack willow, which may reach a length of 15 cm (6 in), are almost consistently light green and lack the lighter white hairs of the white willow. Growing along waterways and in damp areas, crack willow roots which grow in water have a definite pinkish reddish tinge. The twigs of crack willows may grow into a deformed mass known as a *witch's broom*, particularly

The white willow is one of the willows which are grown for timber. It gets its common name from the grey-white colour of the leaves, a feature which is due to the liberal covering of hairs.

The distinctive feature of the crack willow is the audible 'crack' which occurs when one of the small twigs breaks off. These broken-off pieces may begin to grow and ultimately flourish to form new trees.

during the winter months. As with other tree species, some of the smaller buds fail to develop. However, if they are attacked by fungus or an insect, growth starts, but instead of developing normally, the buds grow out together, forming a mass which, with a bit of imagination, is not unlike a broom. Apparently witches were supposed to cause them. Trees with this deformity are able to recover and timber is not affected by the attack.

Second to the white willow in terms of timber production, the crack willow has the distinction of being the tallest species. Where it is allowed to grow to maturity, it can reach a height of 27 m (88 ft).

The willows and sallows, members of the genus Salix, all have catkins which appear in spring. The trees all grow quickly, aided by the constant supply of water in and around the marsh. Male and female catkins are different; the former are bright yellow when they are 'ripe', because of the abundance of pollen.

The goat willow (*Salix caprea*) gets its name because goats used to feed on the fresh foliage in the spring. Scottish folk know it as the saugh and, in Britain, it has the alternative name of common sallow. It is this species which is also called the pussy willow.

Most goat willows are in full flower in March, although they may be seen as early as December. Once fertilised, the seeds begin to develop and are shed from the parent by the end of May. Although the tree is raided annually for its catkins, this only seems to make it grow more vigorously.

Fully grown goat willows are never very tall, reaching a maximum height of 6·5 m (21 ft). The upper surface of the oval leaves is a subdued green; below they are paler. Unlike many other willows, the bark normally remains fairly smooth, but, because of its small stature the timber is of little value. Gipsies used to make clothes pegs from goat willow, selling them door-to-door or at local markets.

The bay willow (*Salix pentandra*) is much less widespread, occurring in the north of England, the Midlands and north Wales. The scent of the leaves, reminiscent of the bay tree, gives this willow its name. This species may only reach bush height of around 2 m (6·5 ft). As a tree, it may reach a height of 20 m (65 ft).

The leaves are rich, smooth and glossy green, slightly sticky on the upper surface. Leaves are of two sizes: small ones are never more than 1·5 cm (0·6 in) long and grow amongst the normal-sized ones, which are about 4·5 cm (1·8 in) long.

Of similar stature to the previous species, the almond-leaved willow (*Salix triandra*), also known as the French willow, reaches a maximum height of 10 m (33 ft). A characteristic of this species is the haphazard flaking of the smooth grey bark which exposes irregular patches of the brownish red layer underneath. It is native to southern Britain and is found in other woodland areas where it has been planted.

The majority of the basically cylindrical-shaped catkins appear in April and May and some trees carry them throughout the summer. The bright yellow male catkins are the most conspicuous, reaching a length of between 2·5 and 6·25 cm (1 and 2·5 in). In contrast, the female catkin may go virtually unnoticed.

A large number of varieties of this species has been developed, making it very variable and difficult to identify. Where it is used in wickerwork, it may be grown in the same way as osiers.

Although not confined to wet areas, nevertheless the grey willow or common sallow (*Salix cinerea*) is the most common of the willows found in these situations. Both twigs and buds have a distinctive black colour and are covered with hairs. Identification is made difficult because taxonomists suggest that there are two species: *Salix cinerea* and *Salix atrocinerea*. This is disputed, however, by some authorities, who suggest that it is the same species responding to different geographical situations. In certain areas, the tree may reach a height of 12 m (39 ft). In other areas, it is no more than 4·5 m (15 ft).

The common and purple osiers may both occur in marshland. The Normans introduced the word 'osier' into the language. The French word *osier* means a willow bed, which is where the French grew their trees: they are grown in similar areas in Britain. Although these two common species grow naturally, there are many other hybrids and crosses which are grown commercially. These willows are valuable because they produce long, supple stems, which have been used for many centuries for basketry. These stems are known as *withies* or *withes*.

The common osier (*Salix viminalis*) usually occurs as a shrub, reaching a height of no more than 5 m (16·5 ft), but where it reaches tree stature, it is seldom greater than 10 m (33 ft) tall. Originally native to the eastern and southern counties of Britain, it has now been cultivated in several other areas.

The leaves of the common osier set it apart from the other willows. Tapering and narrow, they may be up to 25 cm (10 in) long. With silver felting on the underside, the upper dull green surface is much less attractive by comparison. Although the toothed, wavy edges of the leaf are characteristic, accurate identification of the numerous varieties is difficult. This is made worse by the fact that the common osier may form hybrids with virtually every other British species of willow except the white, crack and bay willows.

The purple osier (*Salix purpurea*) is frequently encountered and is also grown for basket work. The characteristic purple colour of the bark gives the tree its common name. The twigs are slender but strong, with either a purple or reddish tinge. The narrow, lance-shaped leaves have toothed margins and are between 7·5 and 15 cm (3 and 6 in) long. Both leaf surfaces are a dull grey-green and the fully grown leaves are smooth, although they are often hairy when young. The purple osier only grows to shrub height, ranging from 1·5-3 m (5-10 ft).

By coppicing hazel, the tree produces a number of thin stems which can be cut and used for a variety of purposes, such as making spars for thatching.

For many centuries, species of osiers have been grown as the raw material for basket-making and the purple osier is one of the most commonly-grown species.

The hazel or cobnut (*Corylus avellana*) frequently grows in the marshes, where its shoots have been and still are used in thatching (see p. 12). It seldom develops into a tree. Although small of stature, its distinctive catkins attract more than a passing glance from both human and animals in spring. For centuries they have been known as 'lamb's tails'. The catkins are already on the tree in autumn, although in their undeveloped state, they are insignificant grey-green lumps. They grow throughout the winter and, by February or March, have developed an abundant supply of pollen which drifts away in conspicuous little clouds as they sway in the wind.

The female flowers, in the form of smaller swollen buds, send out their crimson thread-like structures, which, after receiving the pollen, wither away, although the familiar hazel nut will develop if the flower has been fertilised.

PART III
MARSHLAND ANIMALS
Invertebrates

BECAUSE OF THE HIGH RATE of plant growth, the marsh can support a much higher number of animals, especially invertebrates, than many other habitats. In particular, the tiny plants which float in the surface waters form an abundant food supply for the zooplankton—the tiny crustaceans and larvae of worms, molluscs etc. Marshland invertebrates can be grouped, according to their mode of life, into aquatic and terrestrial species. In some cases, the adult forms are terrestrial and the larval stages are aquatic.

The most numerous and varied aquatic animals are undoubtedly the unicellular Protozoa. They are invariably found in large numbers but often can be seen only under a microscope. The flagellates, such as *Euglena*, are a group of protozoans which propel themselves through the water by the constant movement of whip-like organs which, in the case of *Euglena*, results in a corkscrew-like motion. Another common protozoan is *Vorticella*. Cup-like in outline, it can often be found attached to the surface of plants by an elastic 'stalk'. It feeds on smaller protozoans, which it catches by means of tiny hairs known as cilia. *Amoeba* is another, capable of all the life processes within what appears to be no more than a shapeless blob of jelly. Its food consists of smaller protozoans and rotifers, all of which it engulfs with its body before digesting them.

All other species are multicellular. One of the simplest is the interesting *Hydra*, named after a Greek marsh monster with nine heads, which grew new heads every time its existing ones were removed. Sac-like in shape, *Hydra* has many tentacles arranged around its mouth. *Hydra* is difficult to find, especially if it is attached to an underwater plant, because it contracts when disturbed.

Flatworms (e.g. *Planaria* spp.) live on the undersides of leaves and on stones. They feed on the eggs of freshwater fishes, as well as on smaller animals.

Large numbers of *Daphnia* and *Cyclops* can be seen swimming about in the water, but it is impossible to distinguish their features without a microscope or a good lens because of their size. *Daphnia* is often called the water

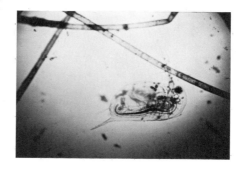

Daphnia, *frequently called water fleas because of the way in which they move, are found in large numbers in various marshland waters. They are a valuable source of food for many other aquatic species.*

flea, because of the speed at which it moves, not because it is related to land fleas. With their hard outer casings, these crustaceans are distantly related to the crabs. Pear-like in outline, the female *Cyclops* is generally more noticeable than the male, as she has two egg bunches attached to the rear of her body.

There are fifteen different British aquatic leeches (Hirudinea), all of which can be recognised by the presence of suckers. A large sucker can be seen at the posterior end and a smaller one at the head end. Apart from their use in movement, the leech also uses these suckers to attach itself to host animals, on which it intends to feed.

Of the numerous marsh inhabitants, the insects—the largest group of animals in the world, containing more than 1 million recorded species—make up the greatest number. Some are totally aquatic, like the water boatman and the great diving beetle, but others, such as the alderfly and mayfly, spend only part of their life cycles in the water.

Of the insects with aquatic stages, the mayflies (Ephemeroptera) occur in some numbers. Once out of the water, as the Latin name suggests, mayflies have only a transitory existence, probably surviving for no more than a day. The short adult life span is compensated for by that of the nymphs, which live in the water for up to 3 years. Large numbers of mayflies emerge at the same time, often in the month of May, as the common name suggests. Once the adults emerge, they have but one purpose in life, to mate, so that the female can lay her eggs before she dies.

Swarming males soon attract the attention of a female. As she flies into groups of dancing males, one will soon attach himself to her and they will fly away to mate. As if the effort is too much, most males die after mating, leaving the female to lay her eggs, usually nearby.

The way in which the eggs are laid varies from species to species: a few place the eggs on suitably submerged objects but the majority drop them as they fly over the water.

The mode of life of the aquatic larvae also varies according to species: some spend their lives swimming; others stay hidden in the mud at the bottom of the water. When fully grown, each nymph makes its way to the surface of the water. It may stay there or it may crawl out onto a plant. As the skin splits, a winged insect emerges. It is not yet fully adult and shortly makes a laboured flight to some resting place close to the water. Another change then takes place which, depending on the species, may occur either in a few minutes or not for hours. The skin again splits and the true adult emerges. Most of the forty-seven British species feed on plants although some may take a proportion of animal matter.

Many of the beetles associated with the marsh are aquatic. The great silver water beetle, *Hydrous* (=*Hydrophilus*) *piceus*, can often be found on water plants or on the muddy bottom of still waters. The larvae are carnivorous and take insects, tadpoles, water snails and small fish but the adults are vegetarian, feeding mainly on plants, including algae. The female lays her eggs in a large cocoon which is placed close to the surface of the water; part of it pushes through the surface film.

The beetle known as *Hydrobius fuscipes* has a series of eleven black spots on each of the wing cases (elytra). It often leaves the water, flying to new areas

The great diving beetle is carnivorous in all its stages. The larva is as vicious a predator as the adult. Both take other water creatures in their predatory attacks.

The adult silver water beetle feeds on water plants, including algae, but the larva is carnivorous, feeding on water snails, tadpoles and small fish.

Superficially caddisflies are not unlike moths. They have two pairs of drab-coloured wings and, although common in the marsh, they are often overlooked because of this. Most species have a liberal covering of hairs. The flight of these insects is rather indefinite and they tend to flutter from one plant to another.

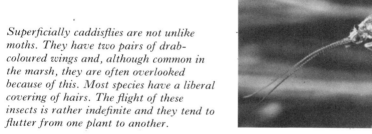

or returning to the same place. Both adults and larvae are predators; the latter often feed on small crustaceans close to the surface. *Enochrus coarctatus* is another beetle which lays its eggs in a silk bag; this is often attached to duckweed. When the larvae hatch they feed on water plants.

The whirligig beetle (*Gyrinus natator*) lives in ponds and slow-flowing streams, where it skims about on the surface in an apparently erratic manner. The paddle-like short hind legs are well adapted for swimming, although it can also fly. Large numbers of these beetles can be seen from June to October; they dive below the surface if they are disturbed. The larvae feed on plant and animal material. Pupation takes place in a cocoon on land.

The great diving beetle (*Dytiscus marginalis*) will be found from February to November, usually in still waters, although it does occur in some rivers and streams. Both larva and adult are vicious predators, taking a variety of aquatic animals. The adults will spend the daylight hours in the water, hunting their food, but they leave at night to fly overland.

Of the ground beetles which occur, *Chlaenius nigricornis* lives in the marsh and around the edges of other areas of water. Predatory in all stages, it takes a variety of other insects. It is locally distributed and can be found throughout the spring and summer.

The larva of the reed beetle (*Donacia aquatica*) burrows into the stems of aquatic plants, including those of the bur-reed. The adult insect has an iridescent sheen, with a greenish head, bronze to brown thorax, and wing cases which have bright green lines around the margins. It is in evidence from March to August; plants growing in and out of the water provide it with food.

In the larval stages, the 150 or so species of British caddisflies (Trichoptera) live in a wide range of freshwater habitats. Many species are of particular interest because of the variety of cases which the larvae build. Using silk from glands situated close to the mouth, the larvae cement together different kinds of material which they find in the water. Some use small stones, others pieces of plant material and yet more take fragments of shells for making cases.

Ensconced inside the case, the larva attaches itself to the interior wall by a pair of hooks. Breathing by means of feathery gills, the caddisfly larva gently undulates its body to create a continuous water current from which it extracts oxygen. The protective case does not seem unduly cumbersome. The head and front legs protrude from the structure. Some larvae swim in search of food; others crawl. All case-building caddisflies are plant-eaters.

Some larvae, instead of building cases, spin nets, using these to attach themselves to the underside of objects, such as stones. Such species are carnivorous and depend on a supply of small creatures being carried by water currents to the nets, which are positioned to face the direction of the water flow. Other caddis larvae, with tougher bodies, do not build cases but move about in the habitat, taking live prey.

When the larvae are ready to pupate, which, in most instances, will be a year or so after the female laid her eggs, those living inside cases cement the case to a submerged object, so that it will not be swept away and then seal the ends. Free-swimming larvae produce a 'case' from grains of sand and, after spinning an internal silken coat, they pupate. When they are ready, they cut their way out of the cases and make their way to the water surface, where they transform into adults.

On land, the caddisfly (the angler calls it a sedge fly) is not a particularly

The large marsh grasshopper has the distinction of being the largest of Britain's fourteen species of grasshoppers. The male performs a song to attract the attention of the female. Once mating has taken place, she lays her eggs deep in the ground, covering them with a liquid which provides a waterproof covering on hardening.

Female alderflies lay their eggs in water, where the larvae will live. Just before pupating, they move onto land. Here they stay for about 3 weeks before they eventually emerge as winged adults.

The china mark moths are the only British moths in which all stages of the life cycle, except the adult, are spent under water. This brown china mark is nesting on a comfrey plant.

conspicuous species. It lacks effective mouth parts, so feeding is generally limited to the taking in of water and nectar. Before death, mating takes place on suitable waterside vegetation. Egg-laying varies from species to species. Some lay their eggs, enclosed in a gelatinous coat, in water. Eggs laid on overhanging plants allow the emerging larvae to drop down into the water. Larvae usually emerge 2–3 weeks after the eggs have been laid.

The dusk-flying nondescript adults are frequently mistaken for moths. By day they remain hidden on waterside plants, including trees. Where cover from vegetation is lacking, they may secrete themselves under stones and logs.

Alderflies, in spite of their fly-like wings, are not true flies, but belong to the same group as the lacewings. The most common of the two British species is *Sialis lutaria* which can be seen around the edges of waterways and ponds and lakes in May and June. They are seldom seen far from water and are uncommon to most people except anglers, who frequently encounter them.

About 2·5 cm (1 in) long, the insect has very dark, heavily veined wings and, although capable of flight, is rather sluggish. After mating, the female lays up to 2000 eggs on waterside plants. The emerging larvae drop down into the water, spending the next 2 years there, feeding voraciously on live food. When fully grown, the larvae emerge from the water and each prepares an oval cell in the mud where it pupates. The winged adults crawl out about 21 days later but they are unable to feed and, soon after mating and laying their eggs, they die.

A number of species of the familiar craneflies or daddy-long-legs lay their eggs in and around water. *Tipula maxima* is the largest in Britain and, typically, is semi-aquatic, occurring around the margins of fresh water and in pools. A rosette of gills at the end of the abdomen allows it to breathe under water, but it will also come to the surface for air. The larva feeds on plant material and comes onto dry land to pupate. The adult flies slowly and suspends itself from vegetation.

The aphid-eating thirteen-spot ladybird (*Hippodamia tredecempunctata*) frequents marshes. Each yellow-brown wing case is decorated with a series of thirteen black spots. The body is less oval than in other ladybirds. Found from April to September, the adults vary in size from 4–7 mm (0·16–0·28 in). The females lay their eggs on aphid-infested plants, which provide both adults and larvae with food. A growing larva may take as many as thirty to forty aphids daily.

The 500 or so different species of aphids in the British Isles are generally termed greenfly or blackfly. They obtain food by sucking the sap from plants and, where they occur in large numbers, they can do a great deal of damage.

Marsh-dwelling female aphids lay their eggs in autumn. The offspring which hatch in the following spring are all wingless females. These produce some winged females, which fly to soft-stemmed plants, where they produce another generation of wingless females. This alternation of wingless and winged females continues throughout the summer. Each female lives for 2–3 weeks and produces at least thirty offspring.

Males do not appear until October. At this stage they and the winged females fly to a suitable plant where they mate and the eggs are laid, ready for the process to begin again in the following spring.

The large marsh grasshopper (*Stethophyma grossum*) is the largest of Britain's fourteen species of grasshopper. It also has the distinction of being the rarest. Fully grown adults measure 3 cm (1·2 in) in length. They are mainly greenish yellow in colour, with red on the hind legs. Adults will be around in the marshes from August to September, seeking out very wet areas with cotton grass and sphagnum moss.

Each grasshopper species has its own distinctive song. It is usually the males which perform most often with the females joining in when they are ready to mate. After mating, the female lays her eggs well down in the ground and covers them with a liquid which, when it hardens, produces a waterproof covering. The eggs remain here until April of the following year when the larvae emerge. Several moults take place before the adult form appears.

Of the numerous moth species which are found in the marsh, some are specifically associated with certain marsh plants, on which the female lays her eggs and on which the caterpillars feed when they hatch. Like butterflies, moths belong to the Lepidoptera, the characteristic feature of which is the powdery scales on the wings.

Several species of china mark moth (*Nymphula* spp.) may be found. The group is unique among British moths, because the eggs, caterpillars and pupae all live under water and only the adults come to land. Although most of the five species which occur in Britain are fairly common, they have, to some extent, been overlooked, possibly because of their aquatic nature and light almost dull colouring. Markings on the underside of the wings are similar to those made by potters on their wares, hence their common names.

They are nocturnal in habit and spend the day resting close to water, coming out as daylight fades. Each female seeks out the underside of the leaves of a variety of floating plants when laying her eggs. On hatching, the caterpillar burrows into the leaves, which provide both food and shelter.

The brown china mark moth (*Nymphula nymphaeta*) lays her eggs on the leaves of such plants as bur-reed and frogbit. On hatching, the caterpillar burrows into the mid-rib of the plant. Later, it uses small pieces of leaf to make an oval case for itself, which it attaches to the leaf on which it is feeding. By moving its body about, the larva creates a current so that it has enough oxygen for respiration. Before pupation, it makes a new waterproof cocoon, which may be attached to a stem or leaf either above or below the water. The adults which emerge can be seen flying between June to August.

The nocturnal slow-flying common beautiful china mark (*Parapoynx stagnata*) is on the wing during the night from July to August. The moth rests by the water during the daytime and is easily disturbed. The eggs are laid on water lily or bur-reed leaves. On hatching, the larva bites its way into the stem. After feeding for a while, it makes a case from two pieces of leaf. It will overwinter in the water and the cocoon in which it pupates is white.

The ringed china mark (*Parapoynx stratiotata*) has a somewhat faltering, fluttering flight and can be seen on the wing from July to August. Females lay their eggs on hornwort and Canadian pondweed; the caterpillar produces a web by spinning leaves and stems together. Body movements produce currents of water which pass over the gill filaments along the body.

The small china mark (*Cataclysta lemnata*) lays its eggs on the leaves of the duckweeds, where the caterpillar makes its larval and pupal cases from the plant's fronds. Both are suspended just above or just below the water surface. The caterpillars hibernate.

In the water moth (*Acentria nivea*), also known as the false caddisfly, the female's wings are either absent or very rudimentary. The winged forms are relatively rare. The female spends her adult life under the water and because of this little is known about her habits.

The male can be seen on the wing from July to September; he flies by night making rapid flights, touching the water from time to time; here mating takes place when the female comes to the surface. The male sometimes carries his mate for a short distance. Between 100–200 eggs are laid on water plants and, on hatching, the caterpillars make cases amongst submerged water plants. Pupation takes place here.

Other moth species feed on the plants in and around the marshland habitat. There are a number of pyralid moths and the crambid moth (*Calamotropha paludella*) is on the wing between July and August. The female lays her eggs on the leaves of bulrushes. The young feed on the leaves and later burrow their way through the tissues. The adults are crepuscular.

In the pyralid moth (*Schoenobius gigantellus*), the hind wings are greyish white and the forewings are much darker, broken up by a series of almost black spots and markings. There is, however, much variation in the wing patterning. When the moth is at rest, the wings are held alongside the body.

This species can be seen on the wing from July to August. It is both crepuscular and nocturnal. It may breed twice in one year, a feature known as *double brooding*. The female lays her eggs on the leaves of reed sweet-grass and reeds. When the caterpillars hatch, they burrow into the shoots of the plants. When a caterpillar has finished feeding on the stem it bites through it and floats to the surface on it. It will then climb onto a new source of food.

Another pyralid moth (*Schoenobius forficellus*) has similar habits to the previous species; the female lays her eggs on the same species of plant and on sedges. The caterpillars bite off the stems in order to float to the surface.

Caterpillars of the reed moth (*Chilo phragmitellus*) burrow into the stems of various water plants including reed sweet-grass and reeds, where they will feed. Sometimes they live above water level; sometimes below. A silken cocoon will be spun inside the plant stem, close to the water level.

Two micro-moths (*Orthotaelia sparganella* and *Glyphipterix thrasonella*) are found in the marshes, the former from July to August, the latter from June to July. *O.sparganella* lays its eggs on the stems of bur-reed and iris and the young caterpillars burrow their way inside. *G.thrasonella* feeds on rushes.

The rosy marsh moth (*Eugraphe subrosea*) was once believed to be extinct in the British Isles but has recently been re-discovered. This nocturnal species is on the wing from July to August. The eggs are laid on sallow and bog myrtle, where the reddish grey caterpillars feed.

The reed wainscot (*Archanara algae*) is a crepuscular species, and the adults are attracted to light sources. Found in marshes and reed-swamps, the adult can be seen in August and September. After mating, the female lays her eggs on the common club-rush. The caterpillars, greenish in colour with black spots, tunnel their way into the stems. They move to bulrush stems when they are ready to pupate.

The locally common bulrush wainscot (*Nonagria typhae*) is crepuscular and nocturnal and can be seen in flight from August to September. Eggs are laid on bulrush stems. The light brown, pink-tinged caterpillars burrow into the plant stem when they hatch.

As its name suggests, the butterbur moth (*Hydraecia petasitis*) lays its eggs on butterbur roots and stems, on which its caterpillars feed. Locally common, it can be seen on the wing in August and September.

Yellow loosestrife, water dock and water mint provide the caterpillars of the water ermine moth (*Spilosoma urticae*) with food. The dark reddish brown hairy caterpillars have a slight purple tinge and single hairs protrude from black spots. The eggs are laid in June.

A closely related moth, the dingy footman (*Eilema griseola*) occurs in July and is crepuscular and nocturnal. The lichens found on alder and willow trees are the food of the grey-brown caterpillars.

The hairy black caterpillar of the reed dagger (*Simyra albovenosa*) has a yellow stripe on each side and along its back. It feeds on reeds and sedge. The quick-flying, nocturnal adults, in flight from June to September, are common in marshy areas and double brooding occurs.

The common pebble prominent moth (*Eligmodonta ziczac*) can be seen from May right through to September, during which time there are two broods. The caterpillar is irregularly shaped, with two pronounced protrusions on the back and another on the abdomen. It feeds on the leaves of willow and poplar.

The osiers in the marshland habitat provide food for the cream-bordered green pea moth (*Earias chlorana*). The name aptly describes the colouring of this nocturnal species, which is on the wing from May to June. The green caterpillar feeds on the osiers.

No other delicate insects are more beautifully coloured than the dragonflies and damselflies and they cannot fail to stir the imagination of the marshland explorer. There are forty-two different British species. Although the adult is dramatically coloured, the greatest part of the creature's life is spent in the nymphal state in the water.

In a strange mating procedure, the male dragonfly clasps the female at the back of the head and they fly together until they find a suitable place for mating. The female bends her body back until she comes into contact with the male's sperm-holding organ and her eggs are then fertilised.

Egg-laying varies from species to species. The female may actually go into the water and, once wholly or partly submerged, place the eggs on underwater plants or the eggs may be dropped into the water from above. In some species, the male retains his hold while his mate is laying her eggs.

This is a dangerous time, as the female is at the mercy of aquatic animals. If she is not killed, there is a danger that she will drown when her wings be-

One of the most handsome as well as the largest insect species in the marsh is the emperor dragonfly. The vegetation in and around water provides it with a hunting ground for its prey, where it hawks regularly. It will prey on other dragonflies.

come waterlogged. The length of time spent in the water by the nymphs after they have hatched depends on the species and may be up to 5 years. Throughout this time, they are predators, feeding on a range of water creatures. The dragonfly nymph has a hinged extensible 'mask' by means of which it catches its food. This is retracted when not in use.

The chitinous skin, which is unable to grow with the body, is shed at regular intervals. Towards the end of this stage in its life cycle, the nymph may swim to the surface of the water and leave it to wander about on land for a short time. In any case, the nymph must eventually leave the water in order to make the dramatic change into an adult. It climbs up the stem of a suitable waterside plant, where the change takes place, often early in the day. Starting at the head end, the skin splits until the creature is able to extricate itself. It then rests for a brief spell, the wing veins filling out as air and liquid is pumped into them. Once its wings are dry, the dragonfly is ready to leave and, after a few fluttering practice flights, it will make off. At first, all the adults have a similar yellow-green colour and it may be a few days before they acquire their distinctive patterning.

The emperor dragonfly (*Anax imperator*) is confined mainly to the southern half of the British Isles, where it is common in south-eastern counties. As its name suggests, it is one of the largest and undoubtedly one of the most beautiful of the British species. In fine weather it constantly hawks for live food; like the nymphal stage, the adult is a ferocious carnivore. It repeatedly patrols the same stretch of land in its search for food, which frequently includes other species of dragonflies. It is on the wing between July and September.

The common sympetrum (*Sympetrum striolatum*) has a much wider distribution than the emperor dragonfly. The adults can be seen from early in July until September or early October.

The southern aeshna (*Aeshna cyanea*), with its strong rapid flight, may be seen during the day from June to October, but also hunts for its food at dusk. Although most food is caught close to vegetation, it does fly higher from time to time.

Hawking for insects by the edges of the water, the brown aeshna (*Aeshna grandis*) is slightly larger than its southern relative. It will be on the wing at any time of the day, as well as at dawn and dusk, from July to October.

The common ischnura (*Ischnura elegans*) is probably the most common damselfly in Britain, especially in lowland Britain, although it becomes less frequent further north. It can be seen from May until the end of August and favours both still and gently flowing waters.

Of the several species of red damselflies, the large red damselfly (*Pyrrhosoma nymphula*) is the most common. Found around still waters, it often comes out before any of the other species. When the weather is favourable, these red damselflies are on the wing from the beginning of May until early September.

The emerald dragonfly, also known as the green lestes (*Lestes sponsa*), is found in many areas and is undoubtedly more common in the southern counties than those further north. This small species exhibits a characteristic green metallic sheen, but is unlikely to be confused with any other, since

Lestes dryas, which is the only species of the same colour, is so rare that it is hardly likely to be encountered. It is a weak flier and generally stays around the edges of water when it emerges in July; it may be seen until September. It usually ventures over the water only when laying its eggs.

Although the marsh fritillary butterfly (*Euphydryas aurinia*) does well in marshy areas, it may be found elsewhere as long as there is a supply of its food plant—the devilsbit scabious (*Succisa pratensis*). A numerous species in the past it reached pest proportions in some areas.

The first butterflies emerge from hibernation towards the end of May. Although its flight is not particularly powerful it displays throughout June and the male often produces more energetic manoeuvres than the female.

The female lays her eggs on the undersurface of devilsbit scabious leaves. The caterpillars, which emerge together, start life by spinning a tangled mass of silken threads, slung between the stems of the plant. After their food supply is exhausted, they move as a band to another suitable plant, first making a new web for protection.

In the autumn, the caterpillars complete their feeding and, having shed their skins for the third time, they make a new web on the same plant at ground level. They stay here through the winter in a state of suspended animation. The caterpillars will stir in spring and may wander about, but should adverse conditions return they will go back to their winter quarters. When ready to pupate, the caterpillar spins a silken pad and, suspended upside down from a stem, it changes from caterpillar to adult.

The swallowtail butterfly (*Papilio machaon*) is undoubtedly the largest and most colourful of the marshland butterflies, with a wingspan of 7·25 cm (2·9 in). The first adults emerge from the pupal state towards the end of May and throughout June. A few adults, the result of early egg-laying by butterflies emerging from the over-wintering chrysalids, will appear in August.

The butterflies go through a particularly stunning courtship ritual, in which a pair of swallowtails takes to the wing. Once airborne, they continue upwards in ever-decreasing circles. Having reached the extremity of their climb, they plunge towards the ground, landing on vegetation, where mating takes place.

Umbelliferous plants are the sole food source of the swallowtail caterpillar. The plants eaten vary from area to area but include fennel, wild carrot and wild angelica. In the Norfolk Broads, the insect's last stronghold in the British Isles, the female searches for the leaves of milk parsley (*Peucedanum palustre*), where, curving her body, she expels a single creamy-white, almost translucent egg. It begins to darken after several hours, becoming purple-brown by the time it is ready to hatch.

The egg normally hatches after 7–10 days and the small caterpillar, black with a white band, resembles a bird dropping. The caterpillar moults four times during the first month and changes colour so that, by the final moult, it is bright green and each segment has an orange-spotted black band. There is a U-shaped tubercle behind the head and this, to deter would-be predators, exudes a liquid which smells like over-ripe or rotting pineapples.

Six to seven weeks after the egg was laid, the caterpillar leaves the food plant and climbs up a reed stem, where it produces a silken thread which it

The large red damselfly is probably the first damselfly species to emerge when the warmer weather arrives, and appears at the beginning of May; specimens can be seen around until August. The larval stage is aquatic and, like the adult, is carnivorous.

The emerald damselfly can be seen flying, when the sun is shining, from June to September. It has a wide distribution, ranging from ponds fringed with reeds to marshland ditches.

The marsh fritillary butterfly is common in the marsh, as its name implies, although it may be attracted to other areas by the devilsbit scabious. Sunshine will draw it out from May to June. The eggs are laid on devilsbit scabious and the caterpillars which emerge are gregarious and spin silken webs when they emerge.

The most striking of the marshland insects is undoubtedly the swallowtail butterfly. The adults first mate in May but a second brood appears in July or August.

The eggs are laid on umbelliferous plants, including milk parsley. After feeding for between 6 and 7 weeks, the caterpillars make their way up the stems of reeds. Securing themselves with silk, they take on a similar colour to the reed stem, effectively camouflaging themselves.

Adult small tortoiseshell butterflies wake from their winter sleep early in the year, looking for nourishment before they mate. They may appear in the marsh, and other habitats, during the winter if conditions are mild.

uses to fasten the bottom part of its body to the reed. A silken collar secures the top half of the body and the caterpillar changes into a chrysalis, often the same colour as the reed stem. It is in this state that the swallowtail overwinters.

The brimstone butterfly (*Gonepteryx rhamni*) frequents marshland areas, where the female lays her eggs on alder buckthorn. It is the male which gives the species its common name because of his sulphur-coloured wings, which contrast with the greenish white scales of the female. At rest, the folded wings are reminiscent of a veined leaf, a protective feature which helps to ensure the butterfly's survival when it hibernates on trees in winter.

The brimstone wakes from its winter sleep early in spring and the female lays her eggs singly on the underside of alder buckthorn leaves. The green caterpillars are well camouflaged on the leaves on which they feed. The new adults appear in late July or early August.

In late March or early April, as the warm rays of spring sunshine penetrate their hibernatory quarters, the small tortoiseshell butterfly (*Aglais urticae*) will wake up. It visits early marshland flowers for a supply of food and, if the occasional patch of stinging nettles occurs, the female may lay her eggs.

The adult peacock butterfly (*Inachis io*) finds a supply of nectar in many marshland plants, such as hemp agrimony and meadowsweet. Patches of stinging nettles, which often occur around the periphery of the marsh, provide both a site for egg-laying and food for the caterpillars when they hatch.

Bumblebees or humblebees (*Bombus* spp.) nest in some of the marshes, especially where the vegetation has been cut for hay. Their noisy buzzing can be heard in the marsh through the summer months. Familiar to most people, their bodies are thickly coated with hair, which, with their large size, makes them particularly conspicuous.

Only the young queens survive at the end of summer and they seek out sheltered spots in which to overwinter. They re-appear in spring and at first make short flights to search for any available nectar.

Once the weather is warm enough, they look for nesting sites, often taking over the disused nests of voles and mice. Each queen collects pollen and forms it into a pea-sized ball, on which she lays 10-12 eggs. When the eggs hatch, in about 4 days, the larvae feed on the pollen.

After a series of changes, the larvae reach the adult stage. All of them are workers (underdeveloped females) and they will help the queen. Males appear at a later stage.

The only aquatic spider, the water spider (*Argyroneta aquatica*) is virtually indistinguishable from terrestrial species. The female is unusual in being smaller than the male and in not exhibiting the aggressive behaviour characteristic of many other species. Both sexes often live together.

Individuals make a web-shaped structure from silk and aquatic plants. After completion, the spider fills it with air which it collects on numerous visits to the surface and it becomes tent-shaped. The spider lives here, making use of the oxygen in the stored air. As it is used up, more diffuses from the surrounding water.

Dead insects are taken from the water surface and carried back to the spider's underwater home where they are eaten. If there are no dead animals, live ones are poisoned.

The female spider lays 30–70 eggs in the upper part of the shelter close to the surface. After hatching, young spiders take up temporary residence in disused snail shells.

Several species of wolf spider live in marshy areas. The swamp spider or marsh spider (*Dolomedes fimbriatus*) is one of the largest northern European wolf spiders. Because of its habit of floating on leaves, it has incorrectly been called the raft spider. Although not aquatic it does run over the water surface when hunting its prey. If danger threatens it will take evasive action by climbing down a submerged plant stem.

The male is between 9 and 13 mm (0·4 and 0·5 in) long; the female between 13 and 20 mm (0·5 and 0·8 in). It is an especially well marked and distinctive species; its brown body is broken up by outstanding bands of either yellow or white. It is particularly active between April and June.

Pirata piraticus, another wolf spider, has a stripe down the middle of the abdomen, as well as unmistakable white spots. The female can be seen in damp situations throughout the year: the male will be in evidence from April to May.

It is an active hunter, as its name suggests. During the day, it may secrete itself in a tube amongst waterside moss. The female carries her eggs with her in a white cocoon attached to the spinnerets, a feature common to all wolf spiders.

Yet another wolf spider, *Arctosa cinerea*, is larger, measuring up to 14 mm (0·6 in). It is found all the year round and will shelter in a silken tube, which is often positioned under a stone. The same home is used during the winter months and the spider remains here even when the water covers it, apparently without any ill effects. It actively pursues a variety of insects which forms its food supply.

Floronia bucculenta belongs to the group of orb web spiders and has the distinction of being able to change the colour of its body. Usually light brown with some darker, often black markings around the edges, there are white markings on the abdomen which change colour. If disturbed, the spider leaves its web and is soon well camouflaged on the ground—the abdomen takes on a dullish brown colour and the white spots shrink, almost disappearing.

Araneus cornutus also constructs an orb web, in amongst plant stems in wet areas, and can be found throughout the year. A signal thread from the web leads to the spider's hideout so that any disturbance warns the spider and brings it out to investigate.

The sheet-web which *Antistea elegans* constructs is often spread across a dip in the ground. Out and about from May to August, it is a relatively small spider—between 2·5 and 3 mm (0·09 and 0·12 in)—but its distinctive orange or bright yellow body makes it a noticeable and attractive species.

Living in amongst reeds, as the second part of its name suggests, the spider *Clubiona phragmites* is also found on other water plants, including sedge. It is a nocturnal species and may build a silken retreat where it spends the day, hunting food at night.

Two major groups of snails are found in and around the marshland environment: those which live in the water and those which are found on

The marsh spider is one of the larger spiders to be encountered in the marsh. Although not aquatic, this species can be seen walking over water. When disturbed, it may actually go under water, crawling down the stems of aquatic plants to do so.

Araneus cornutus *is an orb-web spider which uses the stems of water plants to support its web. It also produces a silken retreat, connected by a silken thread to the web.*

land. Freshwater snails are grouped according to the way they breathe. The pulmonates, those normally found in still fresh water, breathe through lungs and are well represented by familiar genera such as the ramshorn snails (*Planorbis* spp.) and pond snails (*Lymnaea* spp.). In the operculate snails, which breath by means of gills, there is a plate, or *operculum*, which closes the entrance to the shell in a trap-door-like fashion.

Ramshorn and pond snails persist in many ponds with an oxygen deficiency by breathing oxygen from the atmosphere. Ramshorn snails survive at the bottom of a pond because the lung can be used as a gill. Haemoglobin, the oxygen-carrying pigment present in the animal's blood, increases the amount of oxygen which can be carried. The snails feed on algae which they scrape off underwater plants with their horny rasp-like tongues, or *radulae*. As the radulae wear away, they are replaced.

Several species of *Lymnaea* occur in water associated with marshy areas. Large specimens of the great pond snail (*Lymnaea stagnalis*) may measure up to 50 mm (2 in) in height, and have a breadth of up to 30 mm (1·2 in). The thin-walled spire-shaped shell is usually pale brown with irregular banding.

The dwarf pond snail (*Lymnaea truncatula*) seldom reaches more than 12 mm (0·5 in) in height. The thin-walled shell exhibits the same transverse banding as seen in its larger relative. It is not strictly aquatic, but prefers to remain in damp meadows, close to the edges of ditches and streams.

The marsh snail (*Lymnaea palustris*) occurs mainly in marshes and their accompanying ditches, although it may be found in other waters, including rivers and lakes. The banded shell, which may reach a height of 22 mm (0·9 in), often has many encrustations on the surface.

The commonest of all British molluscs, the wandering snail (*Lymnaea pereger*) is found in almost every type of freshwater. Reaching a maximum height of about 25 mm (1 in) the shell shows a great variety of form, although the basal whorl is much larger than that of any other species.

The amber snail spends its time in damp vegetation around the marsh. The extremely thin transparent shell has a glossy surface and varies in colour.

There are four species of the terrestrial amber snail, including the wide-spread *Succinea putris*, which is likely to be discovered in permanently damp areas. Many of the species can be considered amphibious, living both in and out of water. Although there is a variety of shell colour, all are basically yellow and some have a glossy sheen; they are thin and translucent with a number of irregular often indistinct striations. The basal whorl is large in proportion to the rest of the shell, but the spire is relatively short.

The freshwater mussel (*Anodonta cygnea*) lives partially embedded in the bottom mud with its two shells, or *valves*, partially open. An inhalant siphon takes in water containing oxygen and food, and unwanted material is released through an exhalant siphon.

The female lays her eggs in the summer. The eggs are retained within the shells of the female where they are fertilised. After hatching, the larvae, known as *glochidia*, stay within the shells until they emerge in the following spring. They can swim by opening and closing their shells, but if they are to survive they must attach themselves to, and become embedded in, the skin of a fish, where they live parasitically for 3 months. Once fully developed, they can live independently.

The freshwater shrimp (*Gammarus* spp.) prefers shallow running water but may occur in some of the smaller streams which feed the marsh. Its habit of swimming on its side makes the animal especially noticeable. Shelter is important and is provided by stones. When disturbed it will swim around until it finds somewhere to hide.

After mating, the female carries the eggs in a brood pouch. The young are also carried here when they hatch. It is quite common to see the larger male transporting the smaller egg-carrying female during late spring and through the summer.

Fish

WHERE WATERWAYS ARE ASSOCIATED with marshland habitats, fish will colonise such areas and thrive. Which species are found depends on the type of water. Some, such as bream and roach, are very tolerant of adverse conditions, including low oxygen concentrations. Other species, such as pike, are more particular in their requirements, as well as needing good vegetation cover.

Although it is normally found in estuaries and around the coast, the smelt (*Osmerus eperlanus*) leaves these habitats for freshwater early in the spring to spawn and may be seen in marshland waters at any time from February to April. Once spawning is over, the adults return to their original haunts. The eggs have a tacky surface, which enables them to adhere to various underwater materials, including weed. After hatching, the young smelt remain in fresh water until the summer, when they join the adults in estuarine waters.

By far the best known of all freshwater fishes, if only because of its reputed vicious nature, is the pike (*Esox lucius*). Throughout every stage of its life, the fish is carnivorous; the size of the food taken increases as the fish grows. Early in its life, it feeds on small creatures in the water, including copepods such as *Cyclops*. From these, it graduates through freshwater shrimps, progressively larger insects and small fish, including the larval stages of its own kind as well as sticklebacks and minnows, until the adult stage is reached. At this point, still carnivorous, the pike turns most of its attention towards the variety of fish which inhabit the same waters. Eels, bream, rudd and roach feature in its diet, as well as other animals, including small mammals, such as the water vole and some amphibians, mainly frogs.

A freshwater species, the pike manages to survive in many situations and will be found in lakes and ponds, as well as slow-flowing rivers and canals. It needs plenty of cover from weeds so that it can hide and shelter while watching for its prey.

Spawning occurs in April or May and the youngest females are the first to discharge their eggs onto the water weed, where they remain attached because of their sticky nature. Of the large numbers of eggs which are laid, it is likely that many, perhaps the majority, are never fertilised, because the sperm has to pass through a hole in the egg, which closes 30–60 seconds after laying. It is 2 or 3 weeks before the fry hatch and they remain attached to the water weed for another 5 or 6 days by means of an adhesive organ. With plenty of food, the young fish—known as *jacks*—grow very quickly, females outstripping the males. By the end of the first summer, the female averages some 8 cm (3 in) in length. It is 2 or 3 years before she is ready to spawn. Once mature, the female may be pursued by several smaller males, in waters swollen by melted snow or heavy rain.

The basic olive-green colour of the scales is broken up by a series of lighter spots and markings, all effective in camouflaging the fish among underwater vegetation. Pike are seldom mistaken for other fish, because of their somewhat elongated heads and bodies. The snouts, often likened to a duck's bill, are distinctive and the characteristic backward-curving teeth prevent prey from escaping once it has been seized.

A bronze to dark green body provides the tench with good camouflage. The thick powerful tail propels it forward like a torpedo.

The tench (*Tinca tinca*), because it is able to live in waters which have a low oxygen content, is often found in freshwater habitats where other fish find it difficult to survive. Ponds and lakes are its main haunts, although it also occurs in slow-moving rivers. It seeks out weed-infested areas, where it lurks, apparently motionless, its dark-coloured scales blending in well with the plant life. Animal life in the bottom mud serves as food for the tench and it will poke about in the mud, digging up live creatures from a depth of up to 7 cm (2–3 in). It is in this layer that it finds a wide variety of insect larvae, including those of chironomids (midges), dragonflies and damselflies. Molluscs, such as freshwater snails, are also taken.

In unfavourable conditions, such as drought and very severe weather, the tench will spend a dormant period in the bottom mud.

The male tench is mature by his third season. Spawning takes place later in the year than in some species, because the water has to reach a minimum temperature of 18°C (64°F) before the eggs are laid. They are green and the female releases them in amongst vegetation. The young emerge in about 7 days, and feed on a variety of small animals and plants which inhabit the water. Growth of the young is a slow process.

The tench has acquired the reputation for being the 'doctor fish'. It has a slime-covered body and other fish, if unwell, are reputed to seek out the tench and rub themselves against the slimy mucus coating. According to old reports, once an unwell fish has done this it will recover.

There is also a tale that the pike, which takes almost any fish which comes within its range, would never touch the tench because of its alleged reputation. However, this is thought to be a fallacy and pike certainly do catch tench, although they generally leave slow-moving fish alone.

The common bream (*Abramis brama*) is widespread in marshland rivers.

Equipped with a set of effective teeth, the pike is one of the most efficient of the predatory freshwater fish. Although lazy by nature, it has an excellent turn of speed which it can put to good use when catching its prey.

The slimy scales are dark grey on the upper parts of the body, with a definite greenish tinge. The lighter sides exhibit a noticeable metallic sheen and, underneath, the scales are much paler, shading from cream to white.

The common bream lives in stagnant or slow-moving water and may be encountered in lakes, ponds and canals, as well as in rivers. Unlike the pike, which is solitary by nature except in the breeding period, the bream is usually found in shoals.

As the breeding season approaches, the males stake out their territory, selecting areas with plenty of weeds. Here there is often considerable activity and those males which have moved in attempt to keep other males at bay. Spawning takes place at night from May to July. When the sticky yellow eggs hatch, the fry feed on a variety of small organisms, including *Cyclops* and diatoms. As the bream grows, the diet changes until it becomes exclusively a bottom-feeder, taking a variety of small animals. It has no difficulty in sucking these up, because its mouth is specially adapted for this purpose.

As its name implies, the silver bream (*Blicca bjoerkna*) can be identified easily because of its silver scales. A native of rivers in East Anglia, the silver bream has been introduced to other areas of the British Isles. Like the common bream, it prefers weedy areas in either slow-moving or still waters, where it feeds on much the same food as its relative.

Eggs are laid from May to July and are shed by the female once the water temperature has risen to 16°C (61°F). Generally they are released in two or three batches. In the first year, growth is rapid, with the young fish reaching a length of about 10–11 cm (4–4·3 in). At the end of their life span, which is usually about 6 years, they will have reached some 20 cm (8 in) in length. Fully grown silver bream seldom weigh more than 450 g (16 oz).

Confusion often occurs in the identification of the rudd (*Scardinius erythrophthalmus*) because it is often mistaken for a roach. Hybridisation occurs between the two species, adding to the difficulty. The variable nature of the scales also makes positive identification difficult. They range from greenish brown to blue-black on the upper surface. The sides take on a bronze metallic sheen, while the belly is either white or cream.

It lives where it can gain some protection and cover from water weeds and is found in ponds and lakes, as well as in slow-moving rivers and in some canals.

The rudd matures at 3 or 4 years of age and, from then on, it will spawn some time between April and June. The eggs are laid in among the water plants, to which they become attached because of their sticky surface.

When the young emerge from the eggs, after 8–15 days—the exact length of time depending on the temperature and the month in which they are laid— they will feed on many of the small animals found in the water. At first they stay attached to the pondweeds, but they soon become active. It is not known what factors affect growth, but some 3-year-old fish may have reached 20 cm (8 in) whereas others of the same age will be less than half this length. This may be due to their high breeding rate, which results in overpopulation. The adults either come to the surface to feed, or feed midway between the surface and the bottom, taking some of the insects and their larvae. Fully grown rudd feed on small-sized fish.

Although the perch (*Perca fluviatilis*) was found in most marshland rivers

A common inhabitant of many different types of water, the stickleback is a fascinating fish. In spring, the male assumes his breeding colours, exhibiting a bright red belly. Once he has built a nest, he actively encourages a female to enter it and lay her eggs, which he then fertilises.

97

of Britain at one time, it is now less widespread, although still considered locally common.

There are two distinct fins on the back and these, together with its thick scales, usually enable it to be positively identified. Both the back and sides of the fish are basically olive-green, broken by several black vertical bands. The underside is lighter becoming cream to yellow, and the ventral fins have a reddish tinge.

Inhabiting either still or slow- to moderate-flowing rivers, the perch is frequently seen because it does not conceal itself as many other species do, but prefers to live under bridges, along the edges of lakes and under trees. Apart from in rivers, the perch also occurs in canals, ponds and lakes, as well as in gravel pits.

Perch come to shallow water to spawn in April and May. The eggs, which are laid in a long string, are wound around the stems of water plants and sometimes catch on the branches of trees which are in the water. It is not unusual for the female to lay several thousand eggs, which hatch in 7 days.

The fry spend the first days of their lives feeding on plankton near the surface, but move out of sight after a few weeks. The competition for food, a factor which is critical where large numbers of perch manage to survive, determines how quickly they grow. Most probably, temperature also has an influence. An average 1-year-old perch is about 8 cm (3 in) long. Female fish grow more quickly than the males. They mature at 3 years, a year after the males.

If there is a shortage of food, the young which emerge may be eaten. As the young fish are weaned off plankton and are able to take larger food, fish, including perch, sticklebacks, minnows and roach, often feature significantly in the diet.

The ruffe (*Gymnocephalus cernua*) is a small fish, varying in length from 14-25 cm (5·5-10 in) and, although common in the marshland areas of East Anglia, is not found in other places. Even where it does occur, it is not found in all waters which could support it. It is best described as being locally common, favouring either still or slow-flowing waters. Small shoals can usually be seen feeding on the larvae of insects while larger specimens take other fish.

The ruffe spawns from March to May and the small eggs are laid in a string which becomes entangled among vegetation. Once the eggs have hatched, the young grow quickly, feeding on small insect larvae, including chironomids.

The roach (*Rutilus rutilus*) has a definite silvery appearance, with a darker, bluish colouration on the back. The scales on the undersurface are orange. Common in lowland waters, it inhabits slow-flowing rivers, ponds lakes and canals. Tolerant of some pollution, it lives in areas unsuitable for some other species.

By the age of 4 years, roach are ready to breed, although some females may produce eggs a year earlier. Spawning takes place from April to June; the sticky eggs are concealed among thick vegetation close to the edge of the water and large numbers of fish make for such places. When the young hatch, after 10 days or so, they remain attached to the vegetation by an adhesive organ.

The roach is a member of the carp family and, like other members of this family, lacks teeth in the jaws and so the size of food which it can take is limited.

The young fish takes a variety of material, depending on what is available, but its diet is likely to include small aquatic animals, such as copepods, *Daphnia*, diatoms and rotifers. As it grows, it is able to eat larger animals and its diet changes to include various insect larvae, like those of caddisfly, mayfly and midge. Water snails, freshwater shrimps and water boatman will also be taken. A certain amount of plant material is consumed, but whether this is eaten deliberately or accidentally taken in with other food is debatable. However, should there be a shortage of animal food for any reason, e.g. pollution, plants will form a part of the roach's diet. Its adaptability when feeding has made the roach one of the commonest, if not the most common, fish in the British Isles. It is also well distributed throughout most of Europe.

Other features of its adaptable life style include its ability to survive equally well in rivers and ponds, where there may be wide variations in temperature. Man has also encouraged the fish, because it is equally at home in newly dug rivers and old established waterways.

For most of the year, the roach generally lacks the aggressive behaviour of some other freshwater fish, such as the pike. Its docility disappears during the breeding season, however. It often hybridises with bream and rudd.

Two species of stickleback are likely to be found in marshland areas: the three-spined stickleback (*Gasterosteus aculeatus*) and the ten-spined stickleback (*Pungitius pungitius*). As is to be expected, it is the dorsal spines which give the fish their common names. The three-spined species generally has three spines on the back, although there may be as few as two and as many as four. The ten-spined variety has between seven and twelve spines. Both species may be common and the three-spined stickleback occurs in both still and flowing water.

Male and female three-spined sticklebacks can be identified easily during the breeding season, when the male has an unmistakable fiery orange-red patch on the scales of the throat and belly. The back is an almost transparent green and the area around the eyes is blue. At other times of the year, differentiation is not as easy: both sexes exhibit silver scales, with blue ones being noticeable on the upper parts of the head.

Once in his breeding coat, the male produces sticky threads, which come from the kidneys; these he uses for binding together pieces of plant materials to make a nest. He then has to persuade the female stickleback to enter the nest and to lay her eggs. Once this has been accomplished he makes sure that the water in the nest is continually aerated and also protects the fry once they have emerged, remaining on guard and keeping them in the nest for about a week.

Sticklebacks mature and are ready to breed within a year but many fall prey to other fish, including perch and pike; yet more will be eaten by kingfishers and otters. Worms and insects provide the stickleback with most of its food.

The ten-spined stickleback follows a similar breeding pattern, building a nest and guarding the eggs and young, but the belly patch on the male is black.

Amphibians and reptiles

THE WORD AMPHIBIAN MEANS 'double life', a reference to the fact that creatures belonging to this group spend the first part of their life cycle in water and the other part on land. Water is essential to amphibians for breeding and marshland, as well as other areas of water, provides the necessary breeding sites. These sites are fast disappearing as a result of drainage and, even where they still exist, they are often polluted. The effects of pollution are two-fold. Pollution frequently results in the death of the breeding adults and their young and also affects their food supply. Conservationists are concerned by the dramatic fall in the number of amphibians throughout the British Isles. In areas where they were once common—such as East Anglia—they are now becoming much rarer.

Amongst soil and dark-coloured dying vegetation, frogs and toads are extremely well camouflaged. They are often confused with each other, although close investigation will show that the toad's skin is covered with many distinctive warts, which secrete a nasty-tasting liquid to deter predators, whereas the frog's skin is smooth and moist.

The common toad (*Bufo bufo*) will leave its hibernatory quarters as soon as the weather becomes warmer, towards the end of winter, and make for its breeding grounds. It will probably be April before the toad has mated and the eggs are laid. Many toads never reach their spawning grounds. Victims of traffic, they are killed as they make for water. Others are killed by predators, such as carrion crows, herons and rats. Where they do manage to arrive at their breeding sites, large numbers may be found in a single area.

The male, sitting on his mate's back, fertilises the eggs as they are laid. They are encased in a jelly-like substance, but unlike the eggs of the frog, they are in long strings, a double row of small black eggs being visible through the translucent material. Because the spawn is wound around underground plants, it is not seen as often as frogs' spawn, which rises to the surface.

Although the spawn is slippery, some ducks still manage to extract the eggs from the jelly. Fish also take their share. After hatching, the young toad tadpoles feed first on algae and then on pondweeds, before progressing to animal food. A variety of animals will feed on them, including various waders, grebes and ducks, snakes, newts and some species of fish, as well as the larvae of some carnivorous beetles and dragonflies.

At one time the common frog (*Rana temporaria*) was abundant, but over the last two decades it has become very rare in some places where it was once found and, in other areas, it has disappeared altogether. The two main reasons for its decline are the widespread use of pesticides and the disappearance of its breeding haunts, due to drainage of the marshes and the filling-in of ponds. The widespread use of frogs and toads in laboratories may also have helped its decline.

The skin on the upper part of the frog's body exhibits a wide range of colour, from red, orange, yellow, brown to grey; a marbling effect is produced by other colours. By changing its skin colour, the frog can effectively camouflage itself against a variety of vegetation and substrates.

The female frog is the larger and measures up to 9 cm (3·5 in) long, where-

The warty nature of the common toad's body distinguishes it from its amphibian relative, the common frog. This warty skin enables it to blend in well with its environment.

The common frog has a smooth slimy skin in comparison with the common toad. Frogs, returning to their breeding areas, often find them filled in or polluted. For this and other reasons, it is becoming increasingly rare.

as the shorter male is often no more than 6·5 cm (2·5 in) long. After spending the winter hibernating, the frog stirs in February to make its way to the breeding grounds. A particular area of water may attract breeding frogs for a very long time and yet a nearby pool will never be used. No explanation has been found for this. Nor is it known how frogs manage to return to the same breeding sites each year. It has been suggested that the smell of the algae attracts them but this seems improbable considering the distances involved. Furthermore, frogs will return to an area which no longer has any water, such as a filled-in pond. Some naturalists have suggested that they use the sun and stars to find their way.

The male frog always reaches the spawning grounds first, closely followed by the female. The persistent croaking of the male common frog is a sure sign that life is starting to stir in the marsh after the colder months. At the onset of the breeding season, the male develops a horny black nuptial pad on each thumb. Sitting on the female's back, he grasps her with a vicelike hold while she releases between 1000 and 2000 eggs, which he fertilises. His task over, he lets go of the female and may turn his attentions to another.

The egg clump sinks to the bottom of the water and, as the jelly which surrounds the eggs swells, the mass of spawn floats to the surface. Each developing embryo has a food supply in the egg itself, and the jelly serves to keep the eggs afloat and to protect them from predators. The black pigment of the egg absorbs the sun's radiant heat and the jelly acts as insulation.

On average, it is 13 to 14 days before the tadpole is ready to emerge from the egg. An adhesive pad allows the tadpole to remain attached to the jelly after it is released from the egg. It cannot feed at this stage. It possesses external gills, but has no legs and the various parts of its body cannot be seen very clearly.

After a short while, the mouth opens and the external gills shrink and then disappear, to be replaced by internal gills. At first, food consists of algae scraped off water plants but later the tadpole becomes carnivorous, feeding on small aquatic crustaceans.

Gradually, the legs develop and the tadpole becomes a froglet, a perfect miniature of the adult, although it is no more than 1·2 cm (0·5 in) long—one sixth of the size of a fully grown adult. When it is ready to leave the water, it moves towards the bank. The legs are not yet strong enough to carry it on land and so it stays near the bank for a while, often leaving the water after a shower of rain, when the surrounding vegetation is wet, so that there is no danger of it drying up.

The frog is a solitary creature. It feeds on a variety of invertebrates, particularly slugs and snails, although caterpillars, beetles, some other insects and spiders are taken on land. In the water, the frog usually finds a sufficient supply of crustaceans. The frog catches its prey by flicking out its extensible tongue and trapping it.

The edible frog (*Rana esculenta*) is a native of central and western Europe and was brought to the British Isles over a century ago. The first frogs were released in 1837 into an area of fen and two of the Norfolk Broads. Initially 200 frogs were set free in Norfolk. Over the next 5 years, nearly 2000 more were imported, in hampers especially made for the operation. The frog readily established itself and formed breeding colonies. It was introduced to other habitats similar to those in Europe but did not do too well. There was no apparent reason for this lack of success.

The adult edible frog hibernates for the winter, finding suitable sites near the water's edge and in the mud at the bottom of ponds. The young frog hibernates on land, under stones and logs or in crevices.

By the following April, the frog is ready to leave its winter quarters. The male is particularly vocal at this time, although it can also be heard throughout the coming months. Where the frogs form large colonies, they croak in unison and can be heard more than a kilometre away. Small sacs on each side of the mouth amplify the sounds.

The edible frog spawns from mid-May to mid-June. In Britain, the female lays no more than 2000 eggs, although, on the Continent, 10 000 is not uncommon. They are laid in batches of around 200–500, which means that the female can more easily control where she places them.

Tadpoles usually emerge about 10 days after the eggs are laid, although their development depends on the temperature. Some tadpoles will have reached the immature froglet stage after 12–16 weeks, but for some reason development is arrested in others, which are still at the tadpole stage when winter arrives. Some, but not all, die. Those which survive continue to feed and change from tadpole to froglet when about 7 cm (2·8 in) long.

Although it may be 4, even 5 years before it is fully grown, the froglet can breed after 2 years. Once on land, it feeds mainly on terrestrial insects. Hidden in amongst vegetation the young frog uses its extensible tongue to capture its food. The froglet may leap into the air to catch flying insects such as butter-flies, moths and sometimes dragonflies. By adulthood, a wide variety of creatures is taken, including smaller fish and small birds. The prey is gripped by the jaws and held by the forelegs before being pushed into the mouth.

The marsh frog (*Rana ridibunda*), the largest European frog, is not a native of the British Isles; the first was introduced in 1935, when twelve were released into a garden pond at Stone-in-Oxney, near the Romney Marshes in Kent. Some escaped and began to breed in the wild. In the marshland habitat, this frog spawns in ditches and in any available open areas of water, hence one of its alternative names is lake frog.

The variable skin of the marsh frog is particularly attractive. The upper part of the body ranges in colour from olive-brown to olive-green, with a pale streak running along the back. Irregular darker sometimes black spots are distributed over the back which is covered in numerous small wart-like lumps. Specimens kept in artificial conditions lose much of this attractive colouring.

The female marsh frog averages 15 cm (6 in) in length; the male is about 4 cm (1·6 in) smaller. The male has external vocal sacs and develops horny pads on his thumbs during the breeding season. These are used for holding the female while mating.

The marsh frog usually emerges from hibernation early in April. Mating and spawning takes place at the end of May or beginning of June. The female produces several batches of pale yellow spawn, each of which contains as many as 2000 eggs.

The frog is active by day and is fond of basking in the sun, where it will remain for some time unless disturbed. It is a powerful swimmer and catches food both on land and in the water, often while submerged. Because it swal-lows its food whole, the size of the prey is a limiting factor but it will take nestlings, small mice, common frogs and newts.

The males are very vocal, particularly during the breeding season, and will often sing in unison, uttering a 'kek-kek-kek' sound which is followed by a 'croax-croax'.

Britain has three species of newts, two of which are found in marshlands. All are closely related to each other. Confusion often arises between lizards and newts, should the latter be found on land, but the smooth skin of the newts, often punctated by a series of warts, is quite different from the scaly skins of lizards, which are reptiles.

Newts must return to the water to lay their eggs. Although the major part of the newts' lives is spent on land, where they happily bask in the sunshine, too much exposure results in death from excessive water loss through the skin. In marshland, damp undergrowth provides the newts with adequate protection. Like frogs and toads, newts can breathe through their skin, which is a particularly important feature during hibernation.

The great crested newt (*Triturus cristatus*) is also known as the warty newt because of its distinctive wart-covered body. The body is olive-brown in colour with a series of black spots. On the belly, the skin varies from yellow through to orange, broken by a series of black spots. The female is the same colour as the male, but lacks the breeding crest.

The female is some 15 cm (6 in) long whereas her male counterpart measures only 13·5 cm (5·3 in). In exceptional cases, she may reach a length of 17·5 cm (7 in). This newt gets its common name from the crest which the male exhibits during the breeding season. One crest runs the length of the back and another runs along the tail. The liquid produced by the warts is effective against would-be predators, such as hedgehogs, rats, snakes and water birds.

Awaking from hibernation early in the spring, the crested newt leaves its winter home. The colder months are spent in a moist atmosphere under logs and stones. Making its way to water, it is generally ready to breed by the middle of April.

Before mating, various activities take place. The male positions himself beside or in front of the female and bends his tail almost double and vibrates it, creating currents in the water. He gently goads the female with his snout, at the same time moving his tail almost violently. This activity, coupled with skin secretions, apparently stimulate her so that she is ready for mating. There is no body contact as the male releases a spermatophore—his sperm enclosed in a 'packet' of jelly. As this sinks to the bottom of the water, the female follows it until she can position her body over it. By pressing it into her body she ensures that the eggs are fertilised. Before the female lays her eggs, she touches and smells the leaves of the water plants. Satisfied, she lays about 300 eggs, one at a time, pulling a leaf around each one. Sometimes she lays her eggs on pieces of submerged wood or on stones.

The newt tadpoles hatch within 2 or 3 weeks. They are more streamlined than frogs and toads and bear a superficial resemblance to the adult. The only noticeable differences are the feathery gills and lack of legs. Over the next 10 weeks, the majority will change into miniature adults. Any that do not reach this stage before the winter remain in the water in the immature form.

On land, newts spend the daytime hidden and come out at night to feed on invertebrates, such as woodlice, earthworms and slugs. In the water, a variety of aquatic creatures are taken.

The smooth newt or common newt (*Triturus vulgaris*) makes its way to its breeding waters after hibernation. The male soon develops his bright mating colours and a wavy crest which stretches along the entire back and tail. The almost passive female changes little, apart from developing darker but smaller spots.

Mating and the fertilisation of the eggs takes place as in the crested newt. The smooth newt is the most common species in Britain, as its alternative name suggests, and it is an opportunist. Almost any area of water will provide a suitable place for the female to deposit her annual batch of 300 or so eggs.

Reptiles are not dependent on water for breeding but, nevertheless, some species have found a niche in marshland because of the abundant supply of food there.

Although both the grass snake and the adder are found in marshlands,

The smooth or common newt needs water in which to breed. Many newts arrive at their breeding sites as early as February. The male sports an attractive dorsal crest during the breeding season.

their distribution varies from area to area. In spite of the fact that the adder prefers drier areas, nevertheless it does occur in and around marshes. Its main enemy is man, and it tends to vacate areas where there is disturbance, especially of a human nature. However, in very quiet undisturbed places, it may be more common than is at first apparent.

The adder or viper (*Vipera beris*) takes frogs, toads, lizards and some of the smaller mammals, as well as birds. A venomous bite kills the prey before it is eaten.

Before mating, the male adder endeavours to establish his territorial rights in a display referred to as the 'adder dance'. As two males confront each other, they raise their bodies and push against each other. Once a male has chosen a female, he grips her in his mouth prior to mating. The young develop in eggs inside the female (a process known as ovoviviparity) and between 5 and 18 young are born in the middle of summer.

The adder occurs in northern and central Europe, including Britain, and is the most common of the European vipers: in Britain it is the only species of viper. In the north of its range, where summers are short, the young may be born in alternate years, i.e. the young snakes are not born until the year after mating.

The grass snake (*Natrix natrix*) is widespread throughout western Europe and in the British Isles, where it is found from southern England to southern Scotland.

Its food includes frogs, newts and toads, young birds, birds' eggs, small mammals and earthworms. An excellent swimmer, the grass snake may take to the water where it takes tadpoles and fish. Its agility is not limited to swimming and it is able to climb trees once it has gained a hold. It is not venomous and, as it is unable to kill its food before eating it, it swallows its prey alive and in one piece.

Size varies; in the north of its range, the male grows up to 60 cm (24 in) long and the female up to 90–120 cm (35–47 in). In the south, the male

Female grass snakes often grow to twice the length of the males. Although most grass snakes have an olive-brown skin, some young ones exhibit a distinctive orange colouring.

reaches 90 cm (35 in) long and the female up to 180 cm (71 in) long. Although basically indistinguishable, the female is generally broader than the male.

Apart from its bite, which is never very harmful, this snake has no effective defence mechanisms, although, when picked up, some specimens do exude an evil-smelling liquid. Two methods are used to ward off intruders. The grass snake may either feign death or it may writhe and wriggle, snap and hiss to put off its would-be captors.

As food becomes scarce in the autumn, both the adder and the grass snake hibernate. The adder usually starts its winter sleep in October, either in a rabbit hole or in dense vegetation cover. Hibernation may be solitary or communal when several snakes sleep together. It is thought that, once one adder has found suitable winter quarters, the others follow the scent.

The grass snake also hibernates, alone or communally, in hollow roots or sandy banks. The winter's sleep lasts until March or April, depending on the weather. Mating occurs soon after it leaves its hibernatory quarters.

The viviparous lizard (*Lacerta vivipara*) is generally encountered on marsh banks and walls. When the temperature drops in October, it finds a suitable place to spend the winter. Unlike the snakes, it may be tempted out for short spells during its hibernation period, should the temperature rise sufficiently to warm its winter's home. In severe conditions a percentage of common lizards will not survive.

As the spring warmth lures the surviving specimens from the resting quarters, the male will seek out a mate. Rivalry is common among males, who bite and grapple with each other. Correctly speaking, this lizard is ovoviviparous and, in July, the female bears 3–6 young enclosed in flimsy egg

Unlike the amphibian frogs, toads and newts, the viviparous lizard, being a reptile, does not need water for breeding. However, in most marsh areas, there are numerous dry places, such as banks and walls, and the lizard usually frequents these.

cases from which they have to struggle free. The female seeks out secluded hollows for the 'birth' to protect the young lizards from exposure to the sun.

Food is plentiful in the marsh and the lizard may enter the water for aquatic invertebrates, such as water skaters. Various species of marsh spiders also feature in its diet. It catches its prey with its forked tongue, which can smell and taste. The tongue is also used for collecting liquid, as the lizard is very fond of honeydew, the liquid left on plant leaves by aphids.

Although the lizard will bask in the sunshine in places where it will not be disturbed, nevertheless it also enjoys some cover, especially in moist areas of the marsh.

Birds

IN MARSHLAND AREAS in days past, the skies would be filled with a wide variety of 'marsh' birds. Although certain species, such as grebes, the grey heron, Canada goose, moorhen, coot, mallard and mute swan, can still be seen, their numbers have decreased. Other species—the bittern, for example —have become extremely rare or have disappeared as breeding species.

There are a number of bird species which find a permanent home only in marshland areas, whereas some also occur in other places. Of the 476 different species of birds recorded in Europe, nearly half—188 species—are associated with fresh water and many of these are found in marshland.

Birds which frequent the marsh may do so for shelter, to nest, or to spend the winter as visitors. True marshland species have become specialised for living in the marshland environment and are unable to adapt to other situations. Although vast areas of farmland and woods have also disappeared, the proportion is relatively small compared with the area of marshland habitat which has been destroyed. Birds can deal with various setbacks, e.g. the loss of eggs and young, but they are unable to combat the loss of their habitat. It is inevitable that, as further areas of marshland are drained, changed or polluted, the variety of bird life there will diminish.

Each marshland species is adapted to life in the marsh, and some, like the bittern and the water rail, have evolved superb camouflage patterning, so that detection among the vegetation is virtually impossible. Others, such as the moorhen, have long legs, with widespread toes to spread their weight when walking over boggy areas.

The tranquil attitude and elegant stance of the grey heron generally belies its predatory nature. The marshland habitat provides it with a variety of live food.

Feeding adaptations, most obvious in the various shapes of beak, mean that different birds have different diets, thus ensuring that all birds can find plenty of food—at least that was true in the past. Restriction of the marshland and increasing pollution have affected the variety and availability of food. Nevertheless, among the many colonisers of the marsh—both plant and animal—some will be found to satisfy the taste of each marshland bird. Some birds, such as the heron, are predatory by nature, whereas others, such as the coot, are content to feed almost entirely on plants.

Not all birds found in the marsh are totally dependent on it as a habitat. Some, such as the starlings and swallows, nest in other areas, but gravitate towards the marsh if space is available and if there is overcrowding elsewhere.

Although the grey heron (*Ardea cinerea*) cannot be mistaken because of its size—a fully grown individual may measure up to 108 cm (42·5 in) in height—it may be overlooked because it spends much of its time standing silently and patiently in the water, waiting for its prey. With its head resting on its shoulder, it is very difficult to imagine that the bird has quite a long neck. Although it may seem lethargic, when stirred into action, it moves with lightning speed to catch its food. The bill is an effective weapon with which the heron stabs its prey—fish, frogs, rats, water voles and beetles. In the grazing marshes, it will seize moles.

Although apparently fairly sedentary, the heron will move from one area to another and will cover a radius of more than 20 km (12 miles) in its constant search for food. The marsh provides it not only with sustenance, but also

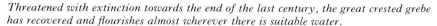

Threatened with extinction towards the end of the last century, the great crested grebe has recovered and flourishes almost wherever there is suitable water.

with breeding sites. It will nest in trees in marsh carrs and heronries may become established in suitable areas. These often expand each year as new birds join.

Before mating, the heron performs an interesting dance, in which the male stretches out his neck, turns it round and bends it over his back. He also brings nesting material to the female, although only she makes the nest. The previous year's nest may be repaired and re-used.

The 3-5 eggs are laid between February to May and will be incubated by both parents for about 25 days. Both parents bring food to the nestlings once they have hatched. It is 7-8 weeks before the young birds are fully fledged and ready to leave the nest.

In 1860, there were only fifty breeding pairs of great crested grebe (*Podiceps cristatus*) in the British Isles and extinction here seemed inevitable. Since then, numbers have increased dramatically and there are now probably more than 4000 breeding pairs. Many reasons have been suggested for this increase, including greater areas of water, due to the building of reservoirs and digging for gravel. This, together with better protection, is probably a large part of the answer.

The great crested grebe inhabits a wide variety of watery and marshy areas, especially where there is slow-flowing water with established reed-beds, which provide breeding sites. The bird has a fascinating courtship display. Pairing takes place from as early as January and displays continue into May. The ritualistic manoeuvres include the offering of vegetation, together with a series of head-nodding and body-raising activities.

Both male and female birds take part in the nest-building and help in the incubation of the eggs, a task which lasts for about a month. The birds cover the eggs with weed when they leave the nest. Both birds share in the upbringing of the nestlings. Young birds can dive after about 6 weeks and attain their independence at 9 weeks. Whilst very young, they may be seen riding on their parents' backs.

Several species of geese visit the marsh to feed. The white-fronted goose (*Anser albifrons*) may be seen from October to April, often descending from great heights.

The first pink-footed goose (*Anser fabalis brachyrhynchus*) arrives in September and is often confused with the previous species. The bean goose (*Anser fabalis*) is less common, but mingles on grazing marsh with other species, including an occasional Egyptian goose (*Alopochen aegyptiacus*). Escapees have established breeding colonies, especially in northern parts of Norfolk.

The Canada goose, (*Branta canadensis*), now our most common species of goose, is a relative newcomer to Britain; the first were introduced about 250 years ago as ornamental water birds. Before very long, some of these large, handsome birds had escaped and were soon breeding in the wild. Now they are found over much of England, parts of Scotland and in Northern Ireland. In Europe, it is also widespread, having originally been introduced as an ornamental bird.

Gregarious by nature, flocks of several hundred birds may be seen before and after the breeding season. In some areas they may breed communally,

The Canada goose was introduced as an ornamental species in the eighteenth century, but escapees established breeding colonies and wild birds now breed freely in many areas. A grazing bird, this goose finds a good supply of plant material in the marsh.

especially in those marshes where there is good grazing pasture close to hand.

As is to be expected from such a large bird—the adult measures about 95 cm (37 in) from beak to tail tip—they are noisy, especially when seeking out mates. There are various courtship displays, the most common of which consists of a neck-stretching ceremony. The nest is a depression in the ground, lined with plant material and covered with down by the female. The off-white eggs, 5 or 6 in number, are laid and incubated by the female for about a month. She tends the nestlings, which leave the nest a few hours after hatching and are ready to fly in about 40 days. The Canada goose is mainly vegetarian and grass features widely in its diet, although small numbers of insects are taken in the summer months. Like other geese, it has been responsible for taking farm crops.

The greylag goose (*Anser anser*) is Britain's only native breeding goose. Flocks may be seen in winter, feeding on water weeds and grasses, although they do take farm crops as well.

The little grebe or dabchick (*Podiceps ruficollis*) is Europe's smallest grebe. It is drably coloured and seen much less often than the great crested species because of its shy habits—it takes to cover at the slightest disturbance. Dabchicks have a courtship display in which sound plays an important part. Positioned opposite each other on the water, the cock and hen birds serenade each other as they stretch out their necks.

Although the most common of the grebes, the shy nature of the little grebe means that it is seen much less often than the great crested species.

A courtship feature which occurs far less commonly than in the great crested grebe is an exchange of weeds. Both sexes build the nest which resembles a heap of weeds. The female lays up to 10 eggs—although between 4 and 6 is average—in April or May.

Arriving in April after a long migratory journey from tropical Africa, the sedge warbler (*Acrocephalus schoenobaenus*) stays in Britain until September. The 'sedge' in its name is something of a misnomer, since the bird is no fonder of this plant than of any other which will provide it with suitable cover when it is nesting.

Once she has found a suitably camouflaged site close to water, the female builds her shallow nest from a mixture of plants, stalks and dried grasses and here she lays 5–6 eggs, which she incubates for about 13 days. Although the male helps, much of the job is left to the female. Both birds provide food for the nestlings which fledge after 2 weeks. A wide variety of insects, including flies, craneflies, gnats, aphids, spiders and caterpillars, make up the diet.

The male and female of the ruff (*Philomachus pugnax*) have different names. The male is the *ruff* and the female is known as the *reeve*. The males arrive at their raised *leks*—exhibition sites—before the females. The males' head tufts are raised before displaying and individuals can be distinguished by their unique ruffs.

Only senior males have permanent display sites; a second group has temporary territories and immature males have nowhere to exhibit. In spite of the ruff's energetic display, it is the reeve which chooses her mate, selecting him by pecking at his ruff.

Four light blue to brown randomly marked eggs are laid in the nest, which

Although many sedge warblers find suitable nesting sites in the reed-beds, others build their nests in bushes and hedges. Its shy nature and drab colour mean it is seldom seen.

is usually on a raised hummock. The reeve alone sees to the chicks, while the male continues his displays. The chicks are independent in a few days. Food consists of a variety of insects, supplemented by worms and perhaps some molluscs, as well as seeds.

In autumn, after the breeding season, most ruffs migrate to an area extending from the Mediterranean through to South Africa. Others are resident and, although the British ruff population remains relatively small, it is protected on the Ouse washes in Cambridgeshire, which ensures safe breeding areas. The bird is widespread throughout parts of Europe. In spite of the destruction of its wetland habitats, ruffs have returned to breed not only in Britain, but also in Norway, Denmark, Holland and Belgium. In France, ruffs breed in the Vendée.

After enjoying a winter sojourn in tropical Africa and Asia, the yellow wagtail (*Motacilla flava*) returns to and breeds right across Europe. Males may arrive up to 14 days before the females. Britain has several wagtails, but the yellow species is more likely to be discovered in marshland areas. Although it generally lives near water, it may also be found far away from it, making its nest and searching for food in very dry areas—arable land, commons and dry heaths, as well as on moorland.

Resplendent in his breeding plumage, the cock is a striking bird, with his yellow eyestripe and forehead. The feathers on the crown and mantle are greenish brown. The white outer tail feathers contrast sharply with the duller black or brown tail. On the underside, the feathers are yellow. The female is drab by comparison, with buff-coloured feathers above and duller colouring on the underparts.

The female makes her nest in a suitable hollow in the ground, which is concealed by vegetation. In marshy areas, she uses a mixture of grass and roots, sometimes substituting straw or mixing it with grass. The nest is lined with hair and receives a clutch of between 5 and 6 eggs from May to July. These are greyish white and have a variety of brown or yellow-buff markings.

They are incubated for 12 or 13 days by both birds, although the female spends more time on the nest than the male. The young remain in the nest for about 2 weeks. There may be a second brood. In some parts of its range, insects, mainly flies and their larvae, make up the bulk of the diet, and caterpillars and beetles may also be eaten. The majority of the insects are probably picked up from the vegetation, although some food is caught when the bird takes to the air on its short quavering flights. Before returning to Africa, family groups come together and roost communally.

Fluctuations in the populations of breeding yellow wagtails causes concern from time to time and, in recent years, there have been instances where birds have either disappeared from areas where they once bred or their numbers have declined.

The majority of rails are marsh birds. The water rail (*Rallus aquaticus*) is shy and secretive and spends the greater part of its life concealed in very damp areas, in thick, almost jungle-like vegetation. Where sparser vegetation occurs, it darts rapidly from one clump of plants to another, defying close observation. The bird is omnivorous and its varied diet includes seeds and roots, as well as numerous invertebrates, such as worms, leeches, crustaceans, insects and molluscs.

Because of its shy nature, and because it is crepuscular, i.e. active at dawn and dusk only, it is seldom seen. Lurking amongst dense vegetation, its presence is revealed only by its calls. Among the variety of sounds which it makes is one likened to a pig's grunt. The intensity of the call belies the fact that the rail is a relatively small bird, measuring no more than 28 cm (11 in) in length. In East Anglia, the calls are called *sharming*.

Because few early writers saw this bird on the wing, many assumed it was flightless. This is not the case and, although its flight is not particularly impressive, most attempts being over in a few minutes, it is powerful enough for it to undertake a migration. Being crepuscular, it migrates at night. In flight, the water rail is clumsy and slow and its lack of manoeuvreability often causes it to collide with man-made objects, such as pylons and telegraph poles.

In his courtship display, the male often offers the female a tempting morsel. She may remain attentive even after mating, temporarily leaving her nest to circle her mate, often stroking his beak with her own while uttering a low call.

The eggs will be laid in a well-concealed nest constructed by both birds from water plants. There may be between 6 and 11 dirty white, almost buff eggs, marked with irregular brown or grey blotches. Incubatory and feeding duties are shared by both birds; the nestlings emerge about 20 days after the eggs are laid.

The hen is sensitive to disturbance and may make herself a new nest close to the old one, if she feels the eggs are in danger. When satisfied, she will carry the eggs one at a time to her newly-built nest.

Although it is infrequently seen, the presence of a water rail will be apparent from its unique and wide-ranging repertoire of groans, which issue from its marshland haunts.

Mainly confined as a nesting species to southern areas of Britain, the reed warbler can be distinguished from the similarly marked sedge warbler by a prominent eye-stripe.

The reed warbler (*Acrocephalus scirpaceus*) and marsh warbler (*Acrocephalus palustris*) resemble each other so closely that they can often only be identified by their calls. It is virtually impossible, even for competent ornithologists, to distinguish between juveniles of the two species. The first migrants to Britain arrive in southern counties at the beginning of May; later, birds can be seen as far north as Lincolnshire and Yorkshire. In the rest of Europe, they breed over much of the continent and in the Iberian peninsula. The males, because they reach their new haunts before the females, spend some time investigating their summer homes. Most seem to have a preference for the common reed, *Phragmites australis*, but where the available nest sites have been used up, due to increases in the population or where more birds have returned, they will nest away from the reeds.

To attract the females, males begin to sing a week or two after they arrive, sitting atop suitable reed stems. Territorial claims, and hence the size of the domain, depends on the area available. In relatively small areas of reeds, there may be a heavy concentration of birds, with 10 or more pairs in half a hectare.

In a particularly attractive dawn chorus, all the birds join in; the concentrated warbling is aimed at attracting any newly-arrived or still unattached females. Males without mates spend a considerable time trying to attract the attention of a suitable female. Once a conquest has been made and their tuneful trilling rewarded, they sing much less frequently.

The nest is supported by reed stems and much of the building is done by the female. Whether she is particularly choosy or whether there is a genuine lack of suitable nesting material remains something of a mystery, but locating enough material for her beautifully-constructed nest often causes her great frustration. Sometimes the female actually takes apart a deserted nest, using some or all of the material to build her own in a different place. Where territories are close, the female may even take to poaching and brazenly steal material which is being used by another warbler. In one recorded instance, a bird carried so much material from a nest in which eggs were already laid, that the nest collapsed!

The nest is woven between two and five reed stems to form a deep cup-like structure. This is lined with soft reed seed heads. As it moves about in the breeze, this shape of nest holds the eggs securely.

A usual clutch consists of 4 or 5 eggs, with greenish white shells marked with grey. During the 12-day incubation period, the bird almost disappears from sight. Once the eggs hatch, the young may be affected by the heat in the cup-shaped nest and the female often becomes exhausted as she tries to keep the young cool by fanning them with her wings.

Although the young may leave the nest 10 days after they hatch, they cannot fly until about a week later. The male may look after the first birds to leave the nest. The almost wheezing call of the young birds is a characteristic sound in the reed-beds where the bird breeds. Reed warblers' nests are popular with cuckoos looking for foster parents for their eggs.

Small birds like the reed bunting (*Emberiza schoeniclus*), which is a close relative of the reed warbler are common. Of the European buntings, this is the most widely distributed. Breeding occurs throughout the continent.

During much of the year, the reed bunting stays close to the marsh, taking its fill of the seeds of plants found there. In the winter, it may seek out fresh supplies of food and move onto fields containing rootcrops and stubble.

During the breeding season, and until autumn, the cock can be distinguished from the hen because of his distinctive black head and throat, which contrasts with the white collar. There is also a characteristic stripe below the beak, not unlike a moustache. In winter, the cock has a more mottled appearance. Characteristic white feathers in the outer tail region are revealed when it spreads out its tail. It is these white tail feathers which distinguish it from the common sparrow.

The reed bunting is just as happy in a meadow with a clump or two of ferns as it is in a dense reed-bed and, with an increase in its population and the disappearance of its habitats, it has tended to move into drier places.

In a period of courtship which precedes mating, the birds chase each other in fast dashes at high speed; such sorties often end with the birds squabbling. The male also attracts the female's attention by puffing up his feathers, which form a collar. Cock birds often mate with several females.

The reed bunting is not very adept at nest-building and the untidy structure is built from dry grass and lined with finer grass and hair. Between 4 and 5 olive-brown or green eggs, with black-brown irregular patches and streaks, are laid. The first brood appears in May, with a second and possibly third clutch of eggs being laid.

The bird's heavy bill deals effectively with marshland plant seeds. Animal food, including insects, beetles, water snails and caterpillars, supplements the basic vegetarian diet, especially in spring and summer. The hen can be seen carrying caterpillars to her early broods. Should danger threaten her eggs or young, the female adopts a broken wing display, which is unusual in the smaller perching birds.

The term 'mute' has only been in use since the late eighteenth or early nineteenth century for the mute swan (*Cygnus olor*) and must be due to some misunderstanding, because the bird makes a series of short hissing sounds if disturbed.

Once a nesting site has been selected close to the water, both the male and female, known as the *cob* and *pen*, take part in the nest-building. He brings her materials, including sticks and reeds, and she arranges them to form the nest, which consists of a large pile of material. Eggs are laid from March to May, with between 5 and 7 eggs in a clutch. The incubating duties last for around 36 days and both adults bring food for the cygnets. The young, still in their dark plumage, often stay in the family group for several months. It is 4 months before they are able to fly.

The marsh harrier (*Circus aeruginosus*) breeds over much of Europe and also in Asia, spending its life in swamps and reed-strewn marshes. Changes in the countryside have greatly affected the status of the marsh harrier. At the beginning of the eighteenth century, it bred in many counties in England and Wales, but some 100 years ago, nesting became sporadic and, by the end of the last century it had stopped breeding in Britain, although it managed to hold on in Ireland until 1917.

From 1908, occasional nests were discovered in Norfolk reed-beds and careful management ensured increasing regularity of breeding until 1927, when the bird began to expand its breeding range. Even so, particularly in Norfolk, the numbers of nesting birds seldom averaged more than six pairs. Others of the species moved to salt water marshes, especially along the Suffolk coast, where breeding occurs at the RSPB's reserve at Minsmere.

The marsh harrier is one of the rarest breeding birds in Britain and, in spite of the optimism which its re-establishment gave to ornithologists, and its recent increases, there is great instability in the marsh harrier population. At one point, coypus were linked with the disappearance of many marshland breeding birds' eggs and, where this mammal was eliminated, harrier numbers did increase. However, like other birds of prey, there is little doubt that pesticides have been instrumental in the bird's decline. Drainage of marshes has also added to the problem.

The marsh harrier is a hawk and, high above, quarters the ground in its search for food. In reed-beds, once the food is spotted, the bird stops and drops to the ground, with long legs outstretched. From a height, the slightest movement in a clump of reeds or disturbance in a pool of water may send the bird on its downward flight.

The marsh is more productive at certain times of the year and, in spring and early summer, frogs, supplemented by young birds, including lapwings and ducks, are taken. Other prey includes moorhens, water voles, coots, grass snakes, young coypu and rabbits.

In Europe, most marsh harriers spend the majority of their lives close to waterways and marshes. Although rare in Britain, its distribution being linked to an ever-decreasing habitat, in some other parts of Europe it can be considered numerous, although drainage activities have decreased the available breeding sites.

More heavily built than most other harriers, its wings are broader and

Mainly confined to reed-beds, the marsh harrier, a bird of prey, has lost many of its former strongholds as habitats have been cleared.

rounder in shape. Both male and female birds have dark brown plumage broken by other colours. The tail is mainly grey and there are areas of the same colour on the black-tipped wings. The male's yellowish brown breast is streaked with darker brown. The female generally lacks the grey of the male.

There is an almost theatrical air about the magnificent courtship display performed by the male. Airborne, he flies up so that he can perform to his prospective mate and, from high in the sky, dives and somersaults his way earthwards.

Most European marsh harriers nest in reed-beds, either raising the structure above a dry area or placing it in the water. The female collects together sticks, reeds and other aquatic plant material and produces a nest up to 60 cm (24 in) across and 30 cm (12 in) deep. Grass is generally used as lining material. Although the male helps his mate in nest-building, he also constructs a platform to which he goes when he is feeding.

The female lays 4 or 5 very light-coloured, sometimes nearly white, eggs any time from late April until June. It takes between 10 and 15 days to complete egg-laying. The 5-week incubation period begins before all the eggs are laid. Conscientiously, the female seldom leaves the nest except to feed. The male provides food, calling her from the nest, and she takes it as they pass in mid-air.

In a large clutch, there may be a few days difference between the emergence of the first and last chicks. They are covered with a pale buff down at birth and grow quickly, feathers soon replacing the down. Both adults bring food to the nestlings. Although the cock bird brings the food he leaves it at the nest and the hen actually feeds the chicks. He may take responsibility for his offspring if his mate is killed and he may manage to rear some of the brood. When weak nestlings die, they may be eaten by the other chicks. Sometimes the nestlings are deprived of food, but on these occasions, the stronger nestlings may allow the weaker ones to have first peck.

The young ones are ready to leave 5 or 6 weeks after hatching, but they are not yet independent. At first, they may experience difficulty in finding a suitable flight path in amongst the tall reeds, because they do not have enough power in their wings. It takes them 2 or 3 weeks to master the aerial manoeuvres. Initially, flight proves frustrating and they will only remain airborne for short spells. The parents teach them the finer techniques of flight and also continue to provide food. Family groups of harriers can usually be seen into late summer or early autumn.

The bird's lifespan is still not accurately known, but is probably quite short. The reason for this assumption is that, although the majority of each clutch is reared, there are always many immature males and, in Britain, they may make up at least half of the male breeding population. Although capable of breeding before they gain their adult plumage, such birds tend to frequent areas occupied spasmodically by mature females. Fully mature birds stay in areas where there are established breeding sites.

Marshy areas provide suitable habitats for many species of duck, both resident and visiting, according to their feeding requirements. Diving ducks need clear areas of water in which to operate. Others, like the mallard, can survive a variety of conditions, provided they can 'up-end' and reach the bottom to search for food. Shallow areas with a plentiful supply of plant food will suit them. Species such as the aptly-named shoveler obtain all their needs from the surface.

Common in marshland, the mallard (*Anas platyrhynchos*) survives in almost any water. Its success is due to its adaptability which has made it the most common of the British breeding ducks. In breeding plumage, the distinctive male stands out clearly against his much drabber mate. The breeding colours appear in October and courtship starts at this time, with the drake taking off and chasing the duck. Back on the water, courtship intensifies with the drake often circling the duck.

The well-concealed nest will be built in any suitable marshland situation; the majority are on the ground, but sound hollow trees are not overlooked. A mixture of grass and leaves is used to construct the nest and it is lined with down. Early egg-layers will have a clutch in February, the latest ones not until May. After laying between 7 and 16 eggs, the female incubates them for about

Found almost anywhere where there is water, the mallard has come to terms with man. The resident population is swollen annually as huge flocks of migratory bird arrive from Europe.

28 days. Exceptionally the drake may take an interest in the ducklings, but generally the duck looks after them. The young birds leave the nest after a short while and fly after 45 days. The greater part of their diet consists of stems and buds and seeds of water plants.

The particularly attractive, green-winged teal (*Anas crecca*) breeds in some freshwater marshlands. Birds weigh between 400 and 450 g (14 and 16 oz) on average. Originally a woodland species, when disturbed it rises almost vertically in the air. Having gained sufficient height, it will take an almost erratic flight path, just as it did in woodland when avoiding the numerous obstacles. When numbers of the birds occur together, they are known as a 'spring of teal', a description which aptly describes the bird's rapid movements.

It is relatively secretive and finds plenty of shelter, as well as a nesting site, in the reeds and rushes; the female lines a hollow in the ground with a variety of dead leaves and her own down. Laid in either April or May, the clutches consist of 8–10 eggs and are incubated by the female for 3 weeks. She tends the nestlings during their short stay in the nest. The young are ready to fly 3 weeks after birth.

A dabbling duck, the bird finds enough food in amongst the reeds, including plant and animal matter. Aquatic weeds and their seeds are supplemented by molluscs, worms and insects.

The garganey (*Anas querquedula*) is the only duck visitor to the British Isles which breeds in the summer. The garganey is similar in size to the teal and, indeed, was described as a 'kind of teale' in the first written record of the garganey in the mid-seventeenth century. It is also called a crackling teal because of the noise which it makes. In Norfolk and Suffolk, it has been called the summer teal. In other areas, including Hampshire, its distinctive, almost cricket-like, chirping has given it the name of cricket teal.

To avoid disturbance, the garganey seeks out dense marshland vegetation. It is more solitary than the teal and British breeding numbers are small. The first garganey reach their British breeding grounds towards the end of March. Many merely stop over on their way to breeding grounds in Scandinavia. Those which stay to breed leave about the middle of October. They feed well before setting off on their arduous journey southwards, most being heavier than at any other time of the year.

The nest is usually built amongst tall waterside vegetation. Various grasses line the basic structure which is finished off with a layer of down. Once the 10–11 eggs are laid towards the end of April or in May, the duck sits on them for 22 days and feeds the young after they hatch. They soon become waterborne, leaving the nest shortly after hatching and taking to the air within a month.

Wigeon (*Anas penelope*) are found in large numbers, especially out of the breeding season, when they frequent mud flats and estuaries. Once virtually confined to coastal regions, riding the waves even in severe conditions, they came ashore to feed on eel grass (*Zostera*), which appropriately has become known as 'wigeon grass'. When the plant was affected by disease, they had to find alternative food and moved inland. On the increase in the British Isles until 60 years ago, the population has since declined and the wigeon is now found mainly in inland areas, although some occasionally nest in coastal marshes.

Ringed British birds breed as far away as the Volga and Icelandic birds make their way to Spain, Italy, England and France, with some crossing the Atlantic to reach North America.

Some of the wigeon's local names have evolved from the drake's almost mesmerising whistling call, haunting and beautiful when emanating from a group of birds, especially in a fog-enshrouded marsh. Several males will often utter this sound as they encircle a female, to attract her attention as they seek a mate. She responds with a quiet, almost cat-like, purring noise.

The duck lines the nest, which is always on the ground, with grass, which she then covers with down. Between 7 and 8 eggs are laid in May and these are incubated by the female for about 25 days. The young will be capable of flight 40 days after hatching.

The shoveler (*Anas clypeata*) is named from its large, distinctive bill, which enables it to feed easily at and from the surface of the water. Vegetable and animal matter is sieved from the water while the bird is swimming; water and other unwanted matter passes out through the comb-like structures on both the upper and lower mandibles.

Shovelers can be seen in Britain all the year, but migratory birds arrive in autumn. After breeding, British birds migrate to France and Spain for the winter. Migrants to the British Isles arrive from Russia and Scandinavia. Shovelers move about in Europe and winter flights may begin as early as August. They tend to concentrate in a smaller area in winter than during the breeding season, with most being found in France, Britain and parts of the Mediterranean.

In spring, before breeding, shovelers take to the air to circle their territory. Once a suitably dry, well-protected nesting site has been found, the duck lines a deep hollow with vegetation and down. Sometimes a 'roof' is provided by the surrounding vegetation. The 8–12 eggs, laid in April or May, hatch after being incubated for 24 days by the duck. The young birds quickly take to the water and eventually become independent, flying after 40 days.

A resident in the British Isles, the common pochard (*Aythya ferina*) population is swollen by migrants from Siberia and northern Europe. In spring, they leave to return to their breeding grounds in Europe. Resident birds begin their courtship display in April. With their breeding plumage, drakes are easily distinguishable from ducks. His head has chestnut-red feathers; hers is more brown. The rest of his body is grey, highlighted by a large, black chest patch. In eclipse plumage from July to September, his back is generally greyer than hers.

A diving duck, the pochard prefers shallow water so that it can reach the bottom when it dives. Food consists of bottom-crawling creatures and the duck also bites off pieces of submerged water plants. From time to time they up-end, a characteristic which is common to bottom-feeders. In the air it is a strong flier and large flocks fly in tight formation.

Like the pochard, the tufted duck (*Aythya fuligula*) is a diving duck. Prior to the beginning of the last century this duck did not breed in the British Isles, although it was common in Europe. As numbers have increased, however, it is now the most common breeding diving duck on this side of the channel.

The black and white plumage is distinctive, with the large white patch on the side of the body contrasting with the rest of the dark feathers. Both duck and drake possess the head tuft or crest which gives the species its common name. The drake's crest is bigger than the duck's and her uniform is more drab than that of her mate. In flight, there is an easily seen white bar on the top of the wing. Bedecked in his breeding plumage, the male stands out from the female. In eclipse plumage from July to October, both birds are similar in appearance, although the male is darker.

Other birds join the British resident population after leaving their breeding grounds in north-east Europe and Iceland. Cover close to the water provides the ducks with nesting sites, several pairs building in the same area. Waterside plants are used for the basic structure and the nest is lined with down from the female's body. Mating takes place after an elaborate courtship display in which the drake holds back his head and whistles softly to attract the duck's attention. To signify her acceptance, she dips her bill into the water and utters an almost jarring call.

The duck lays between 6 and 14 eggs and sits on them for 24 days. She provides food for the ducklings; once in the water they swim and dive competently and will fly after 30 days. Diving for its food, the duck takes plant and animal matter including water weeds, aquatic insects and small fish.

Several other species of duck may turn up from time to time in and around the marsh, although they are far less common.

The pintail (*Anas acuta*) is a nesting species, and the greatest numbers occur in the winter, when migrants arrive from the continent.

There are large numbers of goldeneye (*Bucephala clangula*) in the British Isles, with up to 10 000 birds in some seasons. Arriving in September and leaving in April, a few have mated in recent years. Although many goldeneye remain around coastal estuaries, their distribution is wide and many move

Each year, the resident pochard population is greatly expanded by large numbers of migratory birds. A diving duck, the pochard may spend up to 30 seconds under the water. It cannot generally operate in waters more than a metre or so deep.

The contrasting black and white plumage of the drake tufted duck is highlighted by a distinctive tuft on the head.

It is the nature of the pintail's tail which has given this duck its common name. On the water its long, upright tail is easy to spot.

Bearded tits are affected by our winters. In severe conditions, populations may be driven to the point of extinction. Inappropriately named, the bird does not have a beard, as one would expect, but a distinctive black moustachio.

inland to marshy areas. The goldeneye spends much of its time diving in search of food, often swimming long distances under water.

The gadwall (*Anas strepera*) may be found in marshland areas throughout the year; its numbers increase in the winter, as visitors arrive from the continent and Iceland. A dabbling duck, the bird takes an assortment of aquatic material.

The smew (*Mergus albellus*) is a saw-bill, a name derived from the serrated nature of the edges of the mandibles. This adaptation allows it to retain a good grip on the slippery scales of fish, on which it feeds.

Arriving in Britain in November, the smew departs for its northern European grounds in March. Although the smew does not stay to breed, its courtship activities usually take place just before it departs. The display includes a series of head bobbing movements, as well as the raising and lowering of the head crest.

Its contrasting black and white plumage led the early wild-fowlers to give it the name of white nun. Once in the air, it is a strong flier, although it seems to make hard work of becoming airborne. On land, it appears ill at ease, waddling along with an ungainly gait.

Misnamed in more ways than one, the so-called 'beard' from which the bearded tit or bearded reedling (*Panurus biarmicus*) gets its name is an elongated stripe looking somewhat like a moustache. Although widely distributed over southern Europe, including southern Britain, it is not particularly abundant in any part of its range. The bearded tit relies exclusively on reed and sedge and the plants must be growing in either shallow or semi-shallow waters. With reclamation of its habitats, it has declined throughout most of its European range, with some exceptions, including the British Isles. Once confined to East Anglian marshes, in recent years it has spread to Kent and Essex.

Its decline in the past, led to legal protection being introduced in 1895. This, coupled with cooperation from land-owners where the bird was found, has undoubtedly prevented its extinction.

To attract a mate, the cock bearded tit raises the feathers on his crown and moustache and spreads out his tail feathers in a fan-like arrangement. The female responds by fanning out her tail and prancing about. Sometimes the two birds will then take to the air and fly slowly together.

In thick reed- and sedge-beds, both birds build a nest at the base of reed stems, hidden under dead vegetation, just above ground level. The leaves of both reeds and sedges are interwoven to form a loose structure. The male puts the finishing touches to it by lining the inside with reed flower heads. Once the nest is completed, the female lays between 5 and 7 eggs. They are glossy white or cream, with various thin lines and spots covering the surface. Incubation takes 13 days; both cock and hen birds share the duties. The nestlings will be brought a variety of insects and larvae by both parents. Resplendent in their first full coat of feathers, they become independent after 10–12 days.

Each pair of bearded tits will undoubtedly rear a minimum of two broods and three is quite normal, with four being possible when the summer is prolonged and dry, or when there have been severe winter weather conditions such as those in 1947, 1963 and 1982.

Once the young are fledged, they may wander over a short distance, often accompanied by the male parent for up to a fortnight. Before the last juvenile moult, the young birds pair. Although dispersal takes place during the autumn, ringing has shown that the birds retain this relationship and return to their pre-dispersal haunts to mate and rear their young.

The abundant summer supply of insects and their larvae disappears in winter and the birds turn to the seeds on the reeds for nourishment.

Continental bearded tits have extended their distribution in Germany and Holland as a result of increased populations in the IJsselmeer. The British bearded tit is basically sedentary, but in some of the eastern parts of its range it does migrate when conditions are severe. Where the bird does not move away in winter, it is often affected badly by harsh weather. British ornithologists were very concerned about the Norfolk Broads population in the prolonged cold winter of 1947, when the birds became almost extinct, although they did recover, only to be dealt another devastating blow in 1962–63.

Winter wandering bearded tits were familiar but a strange event took place in 1959. Overcrowding was becoming a feature in the Norfolk reed-beds. As ornithologists watched, they saw large numbers of birds take to the air and circle high over their reed-bed habitat. The birds then left the area altogether, in what was to become the first of an emigratory movement.

Bearded tits were subsequently observed in various parts of the British Isles where they had not previously been recorded. These eruptions took them north to Northumbria, east to Anglesey and south-west to the Scilly Isles. Ringing has shown that these movements are like the migratory habits of other well-known migrants, the birds returning to their original areas to breed.

The bittern (*Botaurus stellaris*) had disappeared completely from the Norfolk Broads by 1850 but has since returned, although its numbers are still relatively few. Drainage projects drove it from many marshes before this, although concentrations occurred in areas which still remained undrained. Although the bittern returned after a 50-year absence, breeding birds were not recorded until 1911.

In past times, country folk were often startled at night as they walked by the marshes and heard, somewhere deep within the tangled vegetation, a booming sound echoing eerily on the still night air. Ill-informed, they believed the sound to be the work of some supernatural being. However, it is the male bittern which makes the booming call which can be heard during the spring. Its strange yet characteristic boom has attracted the interest of man for many centuries. Attempted explanations of the way in which the sound is made have led to many stories. Perhaps one of the strangest was that the bird actually blew through the reed. The boom is penetrating and carries over distances up to 5 km (3 miles).

Hidden in amongst the densest clumps of reeds, the bittern is seldom seen. Although it is related to the heron, the bittern has a short thick neck. The mottled brown plumage is a perfect camouflage in its dull reed- and sedge-bed home. Incredibly, the feathers seem to blend in well with all possible variations in vegetation colour, irrespective of the pose which the bird adopts.

The bittern is one of our rarest birds. It is well camouflaged and normally secretes itself among the reeds, making its presence known only by its unmistakable booming call.

More cautious than the coot, the moorhen is less likely to be encountered in open areas of water, preferring the more sheltered reed-fringed margins.

Coots frequent a wide variety of waters.
They are often quarrelsome and skirmishes
frequently occur as they see off other birds,
which have entered their territory. The
white face-shield is a distinguishing
feature.

In the marsh, the cuckoo lays its eggs in the
nests of the reed warbler. Once strong
enough, the young cuckoo removes the
warbler's eggs from the nest, ensuring that
it will be well fed by its adopted parents.

With a wide-ranging diet, it finds plenty of food in the marsh. Water voles and frogs are supplemented by fish, dragonfly nymphs, water beetles and water boatmen. Infrequently water weeds will be taken. The method used for catching food is akin to that used by the heron. Sometimes slowly, but nevertheless deliberately, the bittern moves through the vegetation or the water. On other occasions, it stands statue-like, the beak poised ready to spear its prey, which is swallowed whole. The serrated bill grips slippery food, such as eels.

In its reed-bed home, the male attracts a mate using his booming call. In dense reed-beds, the female builds a nest from unbroken plant stems, which generally include sedge and reed. These are arranged in a coarse, uneven and somewhat untidy heap and eventually will be above water level. Finer items are used for the lining. The 4–6 eggs are laid between April and May and are well camouflaged by their olive-brown shells. The female sits on them for between 23 and 25 days and, after they hatch, she feeds the young with partially-digested food regurgitated from her crop. Although the male does not come to the nest or feed the nestlings, he brings food to the female. After 2–3 weeks, the young make excursions from the nest, although they do not leave permanently until they are about 2 months old.

The coot (*Fulica atra*) and moorhen (*Gallinula chloropus*) are often confused, although they have quite distinctive features. The moorhen, frequently called the water hen, is one of the most common of our water fowl. It takes its food from water and is found in a wide variety of habitats, including the marsh. Its name at first suggests an association with moors rather than marshes, but 'moorhen' is a corruption of *merehen*, meaning a bird of the meres or lakes.

Although it is at home in the water, it also comes out onto land, where its long spread-eagled feet help prevent it sinking into the mud. In the water, it moves with a jerky action and on land its gait is similar. The forward movement of the head makes the bird conspicuous because of the bright sealing-wax red shield positioned above the beak. As the head goes down the tail goes up, revealing a patch of white feathers. There is a stripe of white feathers on each side of the body which breaks up the drab brown and black.

Once a territory is established, the moorhen will defend it vigorously, keeping intruders at bay. Its saucer-shaped nest surmounts a platform of waterside vegetation. Although most nests are near water, some birds build well away from it and others take to the trees. Between March and July, the female lays a typical clutch of 5–11 red-brown speckled buff eggs. Incubation, by both parents, may last for between 19 and 22 days, with the services of the young of an earlier brood sometimes being enlisted. The young moorhens only spend 2 or 3 days in the nest and, once in the water, they swim and dive well.

Rather solitary by nature, the moorhen inhabits most shallow waters where there is cover from waterside vegetation. When alarmed, and where cover is not close enough, the bird submerges with only the beak remaining visible. The moorhen takes both vegetable matter—water weeds, wild fruits, seeds—and animals—insects, slugs, snails, worms and perhaps the occasional chick or egg of some other waterside bird.

In contrast to the moorhen, the beak and shield of the large coot are white and the feathers a more uniform black. Once it has selected its breeding territory, the coot will do its utmost to defend it. It usually builds its nest in deeper water with good vegetation cover. Both collect together the material to form a substantial platform. In the water, it is anchored for protection, especially against storm and flood conditions.

Between 6–9 buff eggs with black markings are laid from March to May. Both birds help with the incubation, which takes 21–24 days. Both parents bring food. Young coots stay in the nest for no more than 3–4 days. 85% of the food is vegetable matter, but some tadpoles, small fish, newts and dragon-fly nymphs are also eaten.

In the winter, birds from larger flocks often move to the estuaries, especially when inland waters are frozen. When alarmed, a whole group of coots will make for the nearest vegetation cover, kicking up a wall of spray as they go. Like the moorhen, they submerge to avoid detection.

Other birds, seen less frequently, include the common buzzard (*Buteo buteo*), a large broad-winged bird of prey, which may occasionally be spotted over the marshes in its hunt for prey. The rough-legged hawk (*Buteo lagopus*), a relatively rare winter visitor, may be recorded in marshland areas from time to time.

The great cormorant (*Phalocrocorax carbo*) comes to the marsh for fish, mainly in the winter, when conditions around the coast are less favourable. It does occur at other times, however, and immature birds may stay inland during the summer months. Because it lacks oil to protect its feathers, it has to dry itself once it emerges from the water. Cormorants are often seen in the company of the shag (*Phalocrocorax aristotelis*).

Although a rare sighting, the crane (*Grus grus*) occurs in most seasons. A visitor to Britain on its migratory journeys to North Africa, the bird has been recorded in all British counties.

Both the carrion crow (*Corvus corone corone*) and the hooded crow (*Corvus corone cornix*) appear, although the latter's visits are generally confined to occasional winter sorties. Carrion crows, however, nest in the marsh carrs, preying on the eggs of waterside birds, including those of the moorhen.

The cuckoo (*Cuculus canorus*) lays its eggs in some marshland bird's nests, preferring those of the reed warbler, but those of the pied wagtail and the meadow pipit are also used.

Although uncommon, the curlew (*Numenius arquata*) may be seen from time to time, especially on the grazing marshes or nearby ploughed fields, where it eats a wide range of insects and their larvae, worms and occasionally, weed seeds and berries from trees and bushes.

Mammals

THE NUMBER OF MAMMAL SPECIES which inhabit the marshland is much smaller than that of birds. Furthermore, there are no native mammals which are exclusively marshland dwellers in the same way as, for example, the bittern. Those species which do occur, such as the well-known although seriously declining otter, inhabit a great variety of aquatic habitats, although areas where extensive marshlands occur around waterways are undoubtedly popular because of the valuable cover which they offer. Other mammal species—such as the water vole and water shrew—which may be common in the marsh, are not found exclusively in this habitat. Again, drainage and pollution of the marshland affects the mammal population just as it does the invertebrates and birds. In the case of the otter, its very existence is so jeopardised that it is now protected by law in the British Isles.

No other mammal of the marshes can adequately compare with the otter (*Lutra lutra*), which is well adapted for life in an aquatic habitat, with its long, lithe body, webbed feet and muscular tail. The otter belongs to the family Mustelidae and its relatives include weasels, badgers, polecats, stoats and pine martens.

Because of its shy habits and mainly nocturnal nature, the otter has never been easy to study in the wild. Much of what is known about it has been discovered by Philip Wayre, of the Otter Trust, who first bred the animal in captivity at his Norfolk Wildlife Park, but its way of life in captivity is probably not the same as that exhibited by truly wild specimens.

In the water, the otter is an admirable and masterly swimmer, capable of its greatest speed and manoeuvrability while submerged. It has strong territorial instincts: the average bitch otter will occupy a stretch of river 12–14 km (7·5–8·5 miles) long and a dog otter may occupy up to 20 km (12·5 miles) of river. The need for such a large territory is not fully understood. It may be that such a large area is necessary to provide the otter's nightly requirement of 1–1·8 kg (2·2–4·0 lb) of food. When fish is in plentiful supply, the otter will live almost exclusively on this but, when supplies are not so easy to come by, it will turn its attention to other food, including a variety of small mammals and water birds.

Although water is of vital importance to the otter, both for catching food and mating, it is also essential that there is plenty of cover in which the otter can lay up during the day.

When ready to mate, the bitch gives off a scent which, when discovered by the dog, attracts him to her territory. At the beginning of the pre-nuptial activity, the female does her best to deter the attentive male, diving into the water to shake him off. However, there comes a point at which she is ready to mate and does not resist his attention any longer. Mating takes place in the water, after which the male departs, leaving the female to provide the nursery. This is often in a river bank, frequently beneath the roots of waterside trees, such as willows and alder. In lowland areas, it is not uncommon for the female to dispense with an underground nursery, giving birth in a well-concealed bed of reeds in an inaccessible part of the marsh.

She is kept extremely busy once the cubs have been born. What part her

The otter, which inhabits many areas close to water and is superbly equipped for life in an aquatic habitat, is now in danger of extinction. The reasons for this are many and include loss of habitat and pollution.

mate plays in the upbringing is not fully known. He does go to the breeding quarters from time to time and will also take part in excursions once the cubs leave the nursery.

There are 1–3 cubs in a litter. They are blind from birth until they are about 5 weeks old. During this time they are suckled by the mother until they become capable of nibbling away at fish. The proportion of fish in the diet increases, although the bitch's milk is still needed and taken eagerly until the cubs are about 3 months old. At this stage, the cubs are ready to accompany the female on food-hunting expeditions and to catch fish of their own, although they do not become fully independent until they are about 12 months old.

European bats are insectivorous and several species occur in the marshland habitat where they generally find a plentiful supply of food. Most bats are nocturnal and rest by day, hanging upside down but some species may be seen on the wing before dawn and others may be around in daylight.

The majority of European bats are gregarious, including those frequenting marshes, and the colony size varies according to species. The power of sight in bats is not very well developed; hearing is the most important and highly evolved sense. In the dark, the fast-flying bat needs an efficient system of preventing itself from crashing into objects and this is provided by its echo-locating abilities.

As its name implies, the water bat or Daubenton's bat (*Myotis daubentoni*) is perhaps the species most likely to be associated with water and thus with marshes. It is found in other habitats and may live at altitudes of up to 1200 m (4000 ft). It is common throughout much of Europe, except in the south.

Marshland trees may provide summer roosting sites, but if these are not suitable, the bat will search out buildings and walls. As hibernation becomes imminent, it usually moves away to search out attics, caves and perhaps cellars; in some areas it is attracted to rocks. Hibernation lasts from about the end of September through to the following April.

During the summer, the bat leaves its daytime roost about an hour after sunset. With a slow, jerky flight it skims across the marsh, just above the surface of the water. The bat stays on the wing throughout the night, returning to its roost an hour or so before sunrise. In the marsh, insects such as mayflies and caddisflies, form the largest part of its diet. Like other bats, the Daubenton's bat gives birth to one young in June. Blind, naked and helpless, the young bat grows quite quickly.

Daubenton's bat (left) hunts low over the surface of water in its search for insects as food. From time to time, fish may also feature in its diet.

Seeking shelter in woodland areas, the long-eared bat may be found near marshes, where it finds roosting sites in trees and buildings. It feeds on invertebrates, including insects and spiders, and may take these from the leaves of trees.

The pipistrelle (*Pipistrellus pipistrellus*) is common throughout Europe but is particularly so in Britain. Because of this widespread distribution, it is inevitably found in and around the marsh.

The pipistrelle flies high and, although some aquatic insects feature in its diet, it also takes many others. Larger insects are held in the tail pouch until the bat is ready to eat them, whereas the smaller insects are eaten straight away. The pipistrelle averages 7·5 cm (3 in) in length, 2·5 cm (1 in) of which is tail, and flies with a series of quick, albeit regular jerky movements.

It hibernates from about the end of October until the end of the following March. In parts of its range, the creature may not remain in its winter quarters for the whole of this period, but can be seen abroad on mild days.

The aptly named long-eared bat (*Plecotus auritus*) can often be seen along marsh carrs at late dusk. It is found in temperate Europe and is commonly encountered in most parts of the British Isles, although its numbers decrease further north towards the Scottish highlands.

Its summer roosting sites and winter hibernatory quarters are often in the same place; church roofs and beneath the eaves of houses are favourite haunts. Large colonies are usual, with up to 100 bats in a single group.

Insects, including beetles, moths and flies, are taken by the bat, which picks them from vegetation, especially from trees, rather than catching them on the wing. The nocturnal flight period lasts from about half an hour after sunset until around an hour before sunrise. The long-eared bat is active from the first week of April until the middle of October. The intervening months are spent hibernating. Mild spells in the winter may entice the bat out from its winter's sleep.

The natterer's bat (*Myotis nattereri*) may be encountered in some marsh-

The Chinese water deer was introduced to Britain to enhance private collections but it escaped to find new homes, not only in dry, wooded areas but also in wetter marshy habitats.

land areas, where it can be seen searching out a variety of insects, including beetles, some smaller moths and flies. In such areas, mosquitoes probably form an important part of its diet. Food is taken from vegetation as well as on the wing.

Where the noctule (*Nyctalus noctula*) has roosting sites close to marshland, it may be seen at night. It is the largest bat found in the British Isles, although not the largest in Europe. It is widely distributed over much of the temperate part of its European range, although it is not found in Ireland. In Britain, its numbers decrease northwards from Yorkshire. It has been recorded on a few occasions in Scotland.

A native of China and Korea, the Chinese water deer (*Hydropotes inermis*) was first brought to Britain in 1873. Deer eventually escaped from various parks, including Woburn, and there are now wild deer derived from these escaped stock in various parts of the British Isles. Those in the southern counties have managed to adapt and breed in the wild state. The exact status of the Chinese water deer in the wild is not really known, although marshland areas appeal to them because of the available cover, particularly in the wilder areas.

The adult is small in stature and measures between 44 and 54 cm (17 and 21 in) at the shoulder and is nearly 100 cm (40 in) long. Neither sex has antlers and both have elongated tusk-like canine teeth. In summer, the coat is light brown, but it darkens considerably in winter.

The Chinese water deer breeds from autumn to winter. The bucks spend a great deal of time in combat in an effort to prove their superiority and to impress the does. After mating, the doe gives birth between May and June. The breeding activities of the Chinese water deer are unique. Each doe may give birth to up to 7 young at a time, in spite of having only 4 teats, but the average litter size is 4–5. The number of teats is also unique in deer; other species possess only two.

The Chinese water deer is a sociable animal, living in small groups. It is capable of a good turn of speed and, once disturbed, it disappears, moving to cover very quickly. Once out of danger, it drops to the ground, remaining immobile until the danger has passed.

Grasses probably form the basis of its diet, although a wide range of vegetable matter is taken, including some farm crops such as mangolds. The deer, however, is not a pest in any way.

The Chinese muntjac (*Muntiacus reevesi*), which has escaped from the Woburn estate, is sometimes sighted in marshland areas. It is distinguished by its relatively small size; it stands about 40 cm (16 in) at the shoulder and weighs between 13 and 22 kg (28 and 48 lb). Like the Chinese water deer, it is extremely secretive, living in areas where there is good cover, especially in marsh carrs where it can remain hidden. Solitary by nature, this species is abroad during the hours of daylight. Many probably die in the marsh area in harsher winters.

Few people could have foreseen the problems which were to arise when it was decided to import the coypu (*Myocaster coypus*) into Britain. Its coat is commercially valuable, although this might seem unlikely at first sight, and it was persecuted so much in its native South America that legislative measures were introduced to prevent its extinction. Once the value of its fur had been realised, it was soon being exported to various parts of the world, including Britain, and coypu farms were set up. The coypu quickly escaped from captivity and began to breed in suitable habitats in the wild. In England, the escapees soon established themselves in the Broadland areas of East Anglia.

Initially, there was no cause for concern. On the contrary, in some waterways and marshes, the coypu was almost welcomed because it removed weeds and kept the waterways clear. Eventually, however, the Broads were unable to cope with the population increases and severe damage was done to the banks of these waterways and to the reeds, amongst other things. The native wildlife also suffered as the coypu fed on and depleted the available food supply. It was not long before agriculture was also affected, as traditional crops, such as sugar beet, were attacked by the coypu.

After 30 years, moves were made to control the numbers of coypu, which by now had reached pest proportions, and a costly and extensive campaign to eradicate the coypu began in 1962. As their numbers increased, however, new areas were colonised and breeding colonies were established in Cambridgeshire, Lincolnshire and Northamptonshire, as well as those in Norfolk and Suffolk.

Although the coypu can survive harsh conditions, cold winters do deplete its numbers considerably and slow down breeding. The coypu suffers from frostbite as it searches for food. In severe cases, part of the tail or part of a limb may fall off.

The coypu was introduced as a breeding species for its fur. Those which escaped or were released have caused many problems in the marshy areas where they have established breeding colonies. Not only do they cause a great deal of damage to reeds needed for thatching but they may also attack and destroy farm crops.

Although the coypu is mainly herbivorous, it feeds on coarse material, such as reeds and rushes, as well as water parsnips, various aquatic grasses and Canadian pondweed, and the most succulent vegetation is often left untouched. The diet is supplemented by animals, including freshwater mussels and snails.

In spite of temperature variations, the coypu breeds throughout the year, producing a maximum of 2 litters, with up to 9 youngsters in each. After a gestation period of between 110 and 130 days, the young are well developed and are taking solid food after a few days, although they still rely on the mother's milk.

The unusual position of the teats, well up on the flanks, allows the youngsters to feed while the female is in the water. They are weaned about 8 weeks after birth and, although not fully grown, may breed at 3 months.

The adult coypu is about 1 m (39 in) long, with a scaly tail, large head and humped back. The webbed hind feet are successfully adapted for its aquatic habit. Unlike that of many other aquatic animals, the tail is round, rather than flattened. The soft dense grey fur on the underside of the body gives way to a yellowish brown colour above. It is the fur on the underside which has made the coypu so valuable.

Although large numbers of coypus may live close together, the creature is generally solitary, except when breeding. It is especially active from dusk

The water shrew has stiff hairs on its hind feet and tail which assist it in swimming. This shrew has its tunnels along the water's edge and is much easier to observe than the other shrew species.

to dawn and can be heard making a series of growling, some would describe them as moaning, sounds.

Because of its high metabolic rate, the water shrew (*Neomys fodiens*) must be almost continuously active in order to survive. It is mouse-like in shape, but can be distinguished from mice by its elongated pointed snout. Although it is small and short-lived, and caught in large numbers by its predators, the shrew is an ancient animal and has been discovered in fossilised forms dating back to Oligocene times.

The shrew is insectivorous and is continually searching for food. An incredible feature of this active creature is its heartbeat, which may reach almost 1000 beats a minute. Its incessant activity even takes the small mammal out in very cold conditions as it forages for life-sustaining food. Although active throughout the day, it is generally on the move more during the hours of daylight. Periods of feeding are punctuated by resting phases and vice versa!

Water shrews are often found considerable distances—sometimes several kilometres—from the nearest water. Whether they are resident or just passing through is not known. Shrews with established territories seldom travel more than 60 m (65 yd) from their home base, but not all shrews have fixed territories and some seem to wander nomad-like from one area to another.

The majority of water shrews probably live only for a year. Perhaps no more than 1 per cent reach the age of 14 months. The water shrew first mates in mid-April and breeding continues until September. The peak time for activity occurs in May and June. The pregnant female digs out a tunnel in the bank, deeper than the one she sleeps in, and lines it with moss and soft grass.

Occasionally the female weaves a rounded structure from a mixture of leaves and grass. She is ready to give birth about 28 days after conception and there are 5–8 young in a litter. Naked and blind, they are carefully tended by the female for 5 or 6 weeks. Before they are weaned, they live together as a family. This is probably the only time in their lives that they will be sociable, because the shrew is generally quarrelsome and aggressive. Once the young have left, it is usual for the female to mate again, producing a second litter in the summer.

Although it can swim well, the water shrew is susceptible to cold and cannot stay in the water for long as the relatively low temperature soon affects it. It enters the water to catch food and then quickly returns to land. As it dashes into its narrow burrow, the walls squeeze the water out of the shrew's fur, otherwise it would die from exposure. It grooms itself with its hind feet, which are specially equipped with fringed hairs and which comb out any water left in the coat. As the hind feet squeeze the coat, the shrew eats its meal. The fringes on the forefeet are invaluable in the water, helping the shrew to swim. The toes are used like paddles in a boat and the tail forms an adequate, if rather large, rudder.

In the water, the shrew seldom ventures more than 2 or 3 m (2 or 3 yd) from the bank. Under water, the mammal's body glistens because of the air bubbles trapped in the fur. Sometimes it breaks the water surface to seize an insect. It may also walk on the bottom when looking for food.

The water shrew spends its inactive periods in its sleeping quarters, a short tunnel which it excavates. The shrew will be out in all weathers, looking for a supply of food. It sometimes makes short excursions under the ice in its quest for continuous nourishment. Some species eat as much as, if not more than, their body weight in any 24-hour period. It is not surprising that, when it cannot obtain food, it quickly dies.

A shrew's diet is not particularly nutritious. A large part consists of water and indigestible material and the shrew needs to eat a great deal to obtain its energy requirements. The shrew can kill prey much larger than itself, using toxic substances released into the saliva. The creature can kill frogs in this way.

The common shrew (*Sorex araneus*) and pygmy shrew (*S. minutus*) inhabit marshland areas, although they prefer drier habitats, such as marsh walls and river banks. It is difficult to distinguish between the two species. The smaller pygmy shrew, which incidentally is the smallest mammal in Europe, measures up to 8·5 cm (3·3 in) of which 3·5 cm (1·4 in) is tail. The common shrew is 11 cm (4·3 in) long with a tail of 3·5 cm (1·4 in).

Their breeding habits are similar to those of the water shrew; each has 2 litters a year, consisting of up to 10 young. Many will be eaten by predators and the life span of both species is undoubtedly less than a year.

Food consists mainly of worms and beetles, although the common shrew also takes some carrion. Cannibalism, although not a regular phenomenon, is not infrequent. Food must be available all the time, even in severe winters, because shrews do not hibernate. Lack of food results in large numbers of deaths.

The harmless water vole (*Arvicola terrestris*) is often incorrectly called the water rat, probably because its body shape resembles that of the common rat. It is 30 cm (12 in) long, including a tail of 11 cm (4·3 in). The male is slightly larger than the female and weighs about 180 g (6·4 oz) in summer; the body weight drops to about 70 g (2·5 oz) in winter. The short, thick head has a rounded muzzle and the ears are barely visible, gently poking out from the

In the water, the water vole moves effortlessly and quietly, its head and eyes held just above the surface. It comes onto land to feed, taking a variety of vegetation and sometimes climbing onto shrubs to bite off new succulent shoots.

thick fur. The eyes are relatively small and the mammal is short-sighted. The limbs are small and terminate in nearly naked feet. In spite of the water vole's agility and ease of movement in the water, its feet are not webbed but they have stiff hairs on the upper surface and rounded pads on the pink soles.

The vole's grinding molars deal effectively with the diet of rough herbage, but because they wear down they continue to grow throughout the mammal's life. As the top surface of the molars wears away, new material is added to the base and therefore these teeth do not have roots. Across the grinding surfaces, there are sharp ridges of enamel, which extend throughout the whole tooth. A variety of marsh plants provides a plentiful supply of food and includes sedges, flags and many succulent grasses. Where willows grow, the vole relishes not only the young, tender shoots, but also the roots.

There is some controversy as to whether the water vole is strictly herbivorous. It has been seen searching about in the mud looking for aquatic creatures such as caddisfly larvae, freshwater mussels and snails. Collections of snail shells have been found close to water-vole tunnels with the shell at the top of the whorl typically bitten away and the contents removed.

Because the water vole is short-sighted, it is possible to get quite close when it is feeding. However, immediately it is disturbed, it will drop into the water, an unexpected plop giving away its position. Once in, a ripple usually indicates its path. Generally its movements go unnoticed and the creature surfaces some distance from the spot where it entered the water.

Because it has active and inactive periods, the creature was once considered nocturnal. It is usually reckoned to have a 4-hourly rhythm: an active period followed by a resting period, the pattern being repeated throughout the day.

The breeding season spans a period of about 7 months. Some voles mate in April, others not until October. Males sometimes engage in fierce battles, the purpose of which is not strictly clear. They may be endeavouring to establish a territory of their own or they may be fighting over prospective mates.

The siting of the nest varies from area to area. In the marsh, the pregnant female may find a suitable place underneath the roots of a waterside tree—a willow or an alder. If a suitable empty bird's nest is available, she may take up residence there. A mixture of grass and reeds is woven to form a globular nest. Occasionally a male may help the female, although this is the exception rather than the rule.

Gestation lasts for about 3 weeks; 5 is the usual number of young but numbers vary from 2–7. The young voles are naked and blind; their eyes open after 10 days by which time they have also developed a fairly thick coat of golden-red hair. 5 days later they make tentative excursions from the nest but are reluctant to take to the water. They gradually adapt to a new way of life, finding more and more of their own food, so that at 3 weeks they are virtually self-supporting. They also gradually acquire a feel for the water and can soon swim extremely competently.

The young voles soon reach maturity and some will be able to breed in the year in which they were born. Once the young are weaned, the female can devote her energies to further pregnancies and she may give birth to 3–4 litters in a season.

With such a rapid breeding rate, large numbers of voles may occur in the marsh. These 'population explosions' ensure the vole's survival and are characteristic of animals with a short life span.

Younger animals may take over the older voles' territories, forcing their elders to leave. Once away from the cover which the marsh provides, the vole is vulnerable to predators. However, although it is relatively small and apparently defenceless against the attacks of larger animals, the vole does not always succumb easily to would-be predators. Family groups often join in battle to protect a vole when threatened.

There is a peculiar signalling system which alerts the female and young. As a male senses danger, he stands motionless, his snout pointing almost vertically. This stance is taken up by the other males, whilst the female, aware of the meaning of the display, takes herself and her young towards the water. As the enemy approaches, combat commences, with the first male taking up the attack. Once he has had enough and feels he is unlikely to win, he leaves and joins the females.

They have probably taken to the water to avoid the confrontation, but, being inquisitive, return to the bank to watch the progress. A second male now does battle until he has had enough. The attack continues, the logic being that renewed effort and strength will eventually wear out the intruder. When this happens, the combat is over and the enemy retreats. Should the combined efforts of the males be of no avail, one of their number will provide food for the hungry predator! The vole falls victim to many animals, including large trout, eels, pike, weasels, stoats, otters, owls, herons and rats.

The bank vole (*Clethrionomys glareolus*) and the short-tailed vole (*Microtus agrestis*) live in marshland areas. The latter is probably the more common and widespread, particularly in some localities. Population explosions occur from time to time, but these large numbers do not survive for long. Possibly there is not enough food available, or perhaps their predators—including the short-eared owl—take more than the normal quota. Certainly there is an increase in the population of short-eared owls when vole numbers rise.

The bank vole prefers drier areas, for instance where islands occur in an otherwise damp environment. Marsh walls are also favoured. The vole is mainly vegetarian and bark, buds, berries and seeds feature in its diet, together with some insects. The nursery is in an underground nest and here between 3 and 5 helpless naked young are born. In favourable conditions, up to 4 litters may be produced in a year.

Other mammals visit the marsh. The red fox (*Vulpes vulpes*) is almost universally distributed and ever an opportunist and, not surprisingly, it is frequently seen in many marshland areas. The supply of food is plentiful and the fox includes duck, pheasant, small mammals, carrion and insects amongst its prey.

Foxes mate in January or February and 3–6 cubs are born 50–60 days later in the vixen's underground earth, which has a nursery area. In marshlands, the earth is dug in damp areas, although the fox avoids areas which might become waterlogged. The drier areas of reed beds and marsh carrs provide suitable sites. Although generally considered a nocturnal animal, the fox comes out during the day in quieter, more secluded areas.

The rabbit (*Oryctolagus cuniculus*) and brown hare (*Lepus europaeus*) inhabit the grazing marshes. The latter can swim. Rabbit numbers fluctuate according to the ravages of myxomatosis. Although grazing marshes provide both species with plenty of food, rabbits do not generally live in them except where drier areas occur, where they can excavate their underground homes. Hares manage to survive as long as there is somewhere to make their *form*—a surface depression made in suitable vegetation—where 3–4 young are born. Young hares have fur and are able to move about as soon as they are born, so that they are less vulnerable to predators. The female will distribute the young in a number of forms but she does not desert them and makes regular visits to provide milk.

The long-tailed field mouse (*Apodemus sylvaticus*) and, occasionally, the harvest mouse (*Micromys minutus*) frequent the marsh carrs; the harvest mouse generally confines its attention to the drier areas, where tussock, sedges and drier grasses feature. Both species will nest in these areas if conditions are suitable.

The mole (*Talpa europaea*) is frequently attracted to the grazing marshes and often does considerable damage if it occurs in any numbers. It provides a valuable source of food for the heron.

The brown rat (*Rattus norvegicus*) occurs in grazing marshes wherever man lives on a temporary or permanent basis. Holidaymakers in particular attract this scavenger, especially if they leave food about when mooring their boats along the river banks at night.

A plentiful supply of food is available in the marsh for the weasel (*Mustela nivalis*), which lives in various areas but particularly in reed beds and alder carrs. It also inhabits the cover in other areas. The weasel is a vicious predator and, once it has pinpointed its quarry, the fate of the unfortunate creature is sealed. In the sedge-beds, ground nesting species and their fledglings are particularly vulnerable and reed warblers and their offspring will also be taken.

The weasel makes it home in holes and the female rears 2 litters a year, each consisting of between 5 and 10 kittens, born after a gestation period of about 42 days. Blind at birth, their eyes open in 2 weeks. The average lifespan is between 8 and 10 years.

Once the weasel has found a meal, it is loathe to give it up. If it is disturbed it seeks cover, only to return in a short while to continue its interrupted meal. At such times it is not so cautious as it might be and it too may fall victim to one of its predators. Once the young are capable of leaving the nest, they are taught how to hunt.

The stoat (*Mustela erminea*) is often mistaken for the weasel because of the similarity of their long lithe bodies and because their speed of movement makes identification difficult. Apart from differences in length, the stoat can be distinguished from the weasel by the distinctive black tip on its tail. The stoat is 27 cm (10·6 in) long with another 11 cm (4·3 in) of tail. The weasel is shorter—about 20 cm (8 in) long with a 7·5 cm (3 in) tail. Like its smaller relative, the stoat finds a suitable niche in the marshland environment. A ruthless and savage predator, the stoat discovers a wide variety of food in the marsh, taking many helpless fledgling birds, as well as frogs and fish, and eels in the Norfolk marshes. Mammals, up to the size of a rabbit, also feature in its diet.

The stoat mates either early in the year (February or March) or in summer (June or July). After summer mating, delayed implantation will occur; this means that, although fertilisation has occurred, the embryos will not begin to develop until the following year. The litter is born in May or June and contains 2–7 kittens. They are blind at birth but their eyes open after 14 days. The breeding quarters may be found in a wide variety of places—a ditch, marsh wall, any hole or crevice, a rabbit warren—all will provide the stoat with a place to give birth to and wean its young.

Smaller marshland mammals, such as shrews and voles also fall prey to the stoat which seems to have no trouble moving along the runways made by

The stoat, characterised by the black tip to its tail, is often confused with the smaller weasel which does not have such an adornment. A vicious predator, the stoat hunts for birds, rabbits and rats.

the smaller mice and voles. Although generally nocturnal in habit, the stoat does come out during the daytime, especially in areas where it is unlikely to meet any disturbance. Occasionally the weasel may hunt in packs of about half a dozen individuals making a ferociously formidable team.

Feral populations of the American mink (*Mustela vison*) have resulted from escapes from farms and they are now found in many marshy areas around lakes, rivers and streams. Many marsh creatures are taken for food, including frogs, water voles, newts and waterfowl. The mink is solitary by nature and nocturnal. It spends the day in the holes of water voles, which it enlarges for this purpose. It is a competent swimmer and takes much of its food in the water.

THE FUTURE OF THE MARSHLAND

THE FUTURE OF THE MARSH and its inhabitants is not a particularly rosy one. Despite the rich and varied habitat, many of the species are in decline.

A survey carried out by the Royal Society for the Protection of Birds has shown that, of the 109 reedbeds over 5 acres (2 hectares) in England and Wales, 75% are protected, either as nature reserves or because they are managed for commercial purposes. Whilst it is likely that these areas will survive, the remaining 25% is in danger, because unmanaged areas dry out and become colonised by scrub and tree species.

Thus, it is likely that, although some of the marshland areas will survive and retain their rich flora and fauna, the problem of the successful management and conservation of other areas may be too great and too expensive to prevent them from degenerating. Pressures from other sources are also inevitable and many drainage schemes are likely to be proposed and instigated in the foreseeable future.

Intensive agricultural development around the areas of marshland which are left makes great demands on them. Water draining from the marsh dries out the area, bringing about a change in the vegetation and, to some extent, in the animals.

Many of the species mentioned in the preceding pages are typical of, and often confined to, the marsh. Species like the bittern, which have disappeared once and re-established themselves, are again in decline. Fish in the rivers suffer from pollution. Insects, such as the swallowtail butterfly, which rely on plants growing in wetland haunts, find that their terrain is continually decreasing and subjected to abuse from many quarters.

Although the crafts of the marsh still survive—thatching and basket-making, for example—they too have become commercialised. Almost gone are the days of the individual craftsman who was responsible for his work from beginning to end, collected his own materials, made his wares and then sold them himself.

The ways of the people of the marsh have naturally succumbed to the technological innovations of the twentieth century. The wild-fowler has almost vanished and, in his place, wild-fowling, although not yet a sport of kings, has often become a costly pastime as syndicates have taken over large tracts of marshes suitable for wild-fowling terrain.

And what of the future? More than ever there is an increasing awareness of our natural heritage, of the plants and animals which our ancestors cherished, and for which, at last, we seem to have more and more respect. Whether the marsh and its wildlife will survive is impossible to answer. It seems likely that many of the rare plants and animals will inevitably die out, not because of lack of concern, but because that concern has come at too late a stage in their downfall.

The marsh, nevertheless, is still a mesmerising place for the country-lover, especially on one of those rare mornings when every plant seems to be decked with a million diamonds, as droplets of dew cling tenaciously to each leaf and stem. As the gentle sunlight catches them they flicker like a million tiny lights, each breeze moving them and extinguishing their momentary glow.

This is the marsh, pervaded in gentle swirling misty eeriness, with the aromatic smell of water mint drifting on the slight breeze. But such a scene seldom lasts for long, for as the sun slowly creeps over the morning sky, the delicate mist is gradually dispersed and then disappears.

Are we to lose this enchantment, this beauty, this wilderness, with its unique wildlife? Will there come a time when we will never hear the booming of the bittern, or be able to watch the acrobatic courtship display of the exquisite swallowtail butterfly? Who knows what the marsh will be like in ten, twenty or more years time? If it is still a marsh, will it have such a bountiful, intricately-woven web of wildlife? That is not solely for the conservationists to decide, but depends on the delicate balance and interaction of forces which only nature can truly control.

BIBLIOGRAPHY

Arnold, J. (1968) *Shell Book of Country Crafts* Baker, London.

Atkinson-Wiles (1963) *Wildfowl in Great Britain* HMSO, London.

Borgioli, A. & Cappelli, G. (1979) *The Living Swamp* Orbis, London.

Brooks, A. (1976) *Waterways and Wetlands* British Trust for Conservation Volunteers, London.

Brown, A. L. (1971) *Ecology of Freshwater* Heinemann Educational, London.

Bursche, E. M. (1972) *Handbook of Water Plants* Warne, London.

Christianen, M. S. (1979) *Grasses, Sedges and Rushes in Colour* Blandford Press, Poole.

Clapham, A. R., Tutin, T. G., & Warburg, E. F. (1981) *Excursion Flora of the British Isles* 3rd edition. Cambridge University Press.

Clegg, J. (1974) *The Freshwater Life of the British Isles* 4th edition. Warne, London.

Clegg, J. (1980) *The Observer's Book of Pond Life* 3rd edition. Warne, London.

Corbet, G. B. & Southern H. N. (eds) (1977) *The Handbook of British Mammals* Blackwell, Oxford.

Dring, W. E. (1967) *The Fenland Story* Cambridgeshire & Isle of Ely Education Committee.

Dyer, A. (1978) *Basketry – A WI Home Skills Guide to* Berkeley/Macdonald Educational, London.

Ellis, E. A. (1972) *Wild Flowers of the Waterways and Marshes* Jarrold, Norwich.

Harrison, J. (1976) *Wetlands for Waterfowl* Council for Europe Information Centre on Nature Conservation, Strasbourg.

Haslam, S., Sinker, C. & Wolseley, P. (1975) *British Water Plants* F.S.C., Shrewsbury.

Hoskins, W. G. (1955) *The Making of the English Landscape* Hodder & Stoughton, Sevenoaks.

Jones, R. (1971) *Birds of the Norfolk Broads* Jarrold, Norwich.

Jones, R. (1976) *Birds of the Inland Waterways and Marshes* Jarrold, Norwich.

Kvet, J. (ed) (1979) *Ecology of Wetlands* Cambridge University Press.

Mabey, R. (1980) *The Common Ground* Hutchinson, London.

Macan, T. T. (1959) *A Guide To Freshwater Invertebrate Animals* Longman, London.

Macan, T. T. (1973) *Ponds and Lakes* Allen (George) & Unwin, London.

Macan, T. T. (1974) *Freshwater Ecology* 2nd edition. Longman, London.

Macan, T. T. & Worthington, E. B. (1976) *Life in Lakes and Rivers* 3rd edition. Collins, London.

Maitland, P. S. (1978) *Biology of Fresh Waters* Blackie & Sons, Glasgow, Scotland.

Mellanby, H. (1973) *Animal Life in Fresh Water* Methuen, London.

Morris, P. (consultant editor) (1979) *The Country Life Book of the Natural History of the British Isles* Hamlyn, Feltham.

Perring, F. H. & Farrell, L. (1977) *British Red Data Books : 1 Vascular Plants* Society for the Promotion of Nature Conservation, Nettleham.

Tansley, A. G. (1939) *The British Islands and Their Vegetation* Cambridge University Press.

Tansley, A. (1968) *Britain's Green Mantle* 2nd edition. Allen (George) & Unwin, London.

UK Co-ordinating Committee for the Wetlands Campaign (1979) *European Wetlands Campaign 1976–77 : Report for the UK* Nature Conservancy Council, London.

Watson, E. V. (1969) *British Mosses and Liverworts* 2nd edition. Cambridge University Press.

Wayre, P. (1979) *The Private Life of the Otter* Batsford, London.

Whitton, B. (1979) *Rivers, Lakes and Marshes* Hodder & Stoughton, Sevenoaks.

INDEX

Numbers in *italics* refer to pages with black and white illustrations.
Numbers in **bold** refer to pages with colour illustrations.